R.F.

REVELL
ENGLE Roller CAM
Stone
Woods
Cookie
HEADS

# HOT ROD

# MODEL KITS

Terry Jessee

MBI Publishing Company

**Dedication**

To Cynthia—my favorite hot rod model, who's been putting up with all this nonsense for 25 years.

First published in 2000 by MBI Publishing Company, 729 Prospect Avenue, PO Box 1, Osceola, WI 54020-0001 USA



Library of Congress Cataloging-in-Publication Data Available

ISBN 0-7603-0731-8

***On the front cover:*** Some of the most popular early hot rod kits came from AMT and Revell. This photo shows the Revell *Mooneyes* dragster, AMT's '25 *Double T* coupe, and AMT's '40 Ford. *Dan Tilton/Photographic Solutions*

***On the frontispiece:*** Ed Roth's most famous character was the *Rat Fink.* Revell produced several different kits of the famous *Fink*; this particular version is standing on a battery box that powers his glowing red eyeballs.

***On the title page:*** Dragsters have always been a mainstay of Revell's hot rod model kit line-up. Shown are the *Stone-Woods-Cook* Willys, the Thames panel truck, one version of the Tony Nancy *22 Jr.* double kit, the *Mooneyes* dragster, and the *Orange Crate* '32 Ford sedan.

***On the back cover:*** Lined up in front of the local diner is a quartet of hot rod models: AMT's '34 Ford pickup, Monogram's '30 Ford woody, AMT's '25 T chopped coupe, and Monogram's original Deuce roadster.

Edited by Steve Hendrickson
Designed by Dan Perry

Printed in China

# contents

# Acknowledgments

I couldn't have done a project like this without help. This is a thank-you to the great people who contributed to this book with photos, memories, model kits, magazines, and lots of time.

**The National Model Car Builders' Museum:** First, I want to thank the Board of Directors of the National Model Car Builders' Museum in Salt Lake City, Utah: Mark Gustavson, founder and curator; Mark Benton; Mike Barlow; Rex Barden; and Randy Van Draiss. Although it's small, the museum is a wonderful source of historical information. Through the efforts of Mark Gustavson and his supporters, a number of important feature models from 1960s model magazines have been preserved and restored. In addition, the museum has developed a comprehensive research file of magazines, photos, advertisements, and factory documents. Their assistance was priceless.

**The Designers, Engineers, and R&D People:** These are just a few of the hundreds of people who developed the kits and models featured in this book. My thanks to them for taking time to reminisce about their experiences. AMT: John Mueller and Dave Carlock; Revell: Jim Keeler and Bob Paeth; Monogram: Roger Harney; MPC: George Toteff and Bill DePuy; Aurora: Tom West; Lindberg: Larry Perkins.

**The Model Companies and Magazines:** In this age of trademarks and copyrights, these model companies and publishers graciously allowed me to use their logos, advertisements, catalogs, box art, and designs to produce this book. AMT/Ertl: Jim Walsh and Tom Haverland; Revell/Monogram: Ed Sexton, Mike DeLille, and Dean Milano; Lindberg: Matt Thrasher; Petersen Publishing: Lisa Spencer and Jeff Tann.

**The Writers:** This hobby has a remarkable cadre of writers, some of whom have been writing for 40 years. Others, like me, are the kids who grew up reading *Rod & Custom* and *Car Model* magazines. Over the last 20 years, that second group has taken up the task of building and writing to teach a whole new generation how to build better car models. Their work appears in magazines such as *Scale Auto Enthusiast, Car Modeler, Street Rodder, Custom Rodder, Plastic Fanatic,* and *Model Car Journal.* A number of them contributed to this project. They are: Bill Coulter, Dennis Doty, William Bozgan, Mark Gustavson, Bob Wick, Rick Hanmore, Don Emmons, Oscar Koveleski, Ken Hamilton, Jim Keeler, and Bob Paeth.

**The "Big Car" Guys:** Much of this hobby's success can be attributed to the customizers and designers who built the fabulous full-size cars that appeared in *Rod & Custom, Hot Rod, Car Craft,* and other magazines of the era. All of them were gracious and helpful, and they offered some great stories about their exploits with the model companies. My thanks to George Barris, Ed "Big Daddy" Roth, Darryl Starbird, and Tom Daniel. Daniel was especially helpful and provided photos from his personal archives for the Monogram chapter. As you'll see later, Ed Roth contributed his own version of history for the Revell chapter. He's still a blast.

**The Modelers:** These guys, like me, continue to build hot rod models today. Many of the photographs in this book are of models from their own collections. In addition, a number of friends both old and new helped me find rare kits, magazines, advertisements, and catalogs.

Special appreciation goes to Augie Hiscano, Terry Thormahlen, Rod Wagner, Vaughn Kemph, John Bowman, Barry Payne, Jerry Shoger, Randy Van Draiss, Dennis Oberlander, Roby Banfield, Bob Berube, Curtis Hutton, Phil Davis, Mark Abrahamson, Lee Kirchner, Ted Kellison, Thomas Voehringer, and most especially to Bobby Bennett, who had the amazing ability to find exactly what I needed exactly when I needed it. I also want to thank Ed Wright for letting me into his remarkable basement to photograph some real treasures.

**The Model Builders:** These superb craftsmen produced the finished models that appear in this book.

Roby Banfield: Revell *Mysterion*

Bobby Bennett: AMT 1937 Chevy coupe; Revell 22JR dragster (silver); Monogram *Li'l T*

Bob Berube: Revell 1951 Anglia

John Bowman: AMT 1950 Mercury; Monogram 1932 Ford *Drag Strip Hot Rod*; MPC *Milner Coupe*; IMC Volkswagen Gasser

William Bozgan: Revell *Outlaw*; MPC 1970 Mercury Cyclone

Kenny Collins: IMC Dodge *Li'l Red Wagon*

Bill Coulter: AMT Garlits *Wynn's Jammer*; Monogram *Hurst Hairy Olds*, 49ers Fiat coupe; MPC Plymouth *Mopar Missile*; Hawk Weirdos *Digger*

Dennis Doty: Monogram *Sizzler*, 1930 Ford Touring custom

Mark Gustavson: Monogram *Predicta*, 1936 Ford coupe

Rick Hanmore: AMT 1963 Buick, 1925 *Double T* roadster, 1957 Chevy, 1957 Ford; Monogram *Slingshot* dragster; MPC *Wild Ones* 1928 Ford woody; Hawk *Surf Wagon*; Aurora 1922 *T for Two*

Ted Kellison: AMT 1934 Ford pickup (with fenders); Revell 1940 Willys coupe, 22JR roadster (red), *Mooneyes* dragster

Vaughn Kemph: Revell 1932 Ford *Orange Crate*

Chuck Munson: Revell Thames panel truck

Barry Payne: MPC *Ramchargers* dragster, Willy Borsch *Winged Express*, Mr. Gasket Mustang, *More American Graffiti* dragster

Jerry Shoger: AMT 1940 Ford coupe, 1939 Ford sedan

John White: AMT 1953 Ford pickup

Ed Wright: AMT Pirahna; Revell *Drag Nut*, *Rat Finks*; Monogram Deuce *Sport Coupe*, 1940 Ford pickup; Aurora 1934 Fords

In addition, the author built the following models: AMT 1932 Ford coupe and roadster; 1934 Ford pickup (highboy); 1937 Chevy cabriolet; 1940 Willys pickup; 1957 Thunderbirds; *Munsters* Coach, *Dragula*; Revell *Surfite* & *Tiki Hut*; Monogram 1930 Ford phaeton; 1930 Ford woody; 1929 Ford pickup; MPC Switchers 1932 Ford roadster; *Monkeemobile*, *Beverly Hillbillies* truck; *Jolly Rodger*; Lindberg Tee Wagon. For those models not listed, we regret that we were unable to identify a builder.

Finally, my sincere thanks to Jim Eschleman of Kasper's Photo, and to Michael Cruzan and Dan Tilton of Photographic Solutions in Billings, Montana, for their able assistance with photo and film questions. They pulled off some great film magic.

In 1997, the National Model Car Builders' Museum seized a rare opportunity to photograph Revell's 1963 and 1964 national model car champions alongside the executives who ran the contest. From left is Jim Keeler, Revell's R&D director (1961-64); 1963 champion Richard Johnson (Mike); 1964 champion Augie Hiscano; and Bob Paeth, R&D director from 1964 to 1969. Johnson and Hiscano are shown holding their original winning models. Behind them is Mark Gustavson, founder and curator of the Museum. *Collection of Mark Gustavson*

# Introduction

From the mid-1950s to the early 1970s, model car kits were one of the quintessential boys' toys. In that time, the hobby and the industry grew with astounding speed. Bill Neumann, the editor of *Rod & Custom* magazine from 1960 to 1966, once wrote that model companies sold about $6,000,000 worth of model car kits in 1956. By 1964, that figure had increased to more than $150,000,000. Few serious car enthusiasts grew up without at least one or two model kits, and today's auto design studios and racecar cockpits are full of people who started out building model cars.

Model car builders have always enjoyed a creative freedom not available to builders of other types of models. "Why hot rod models?" some readers might ask. "Why not discuss other car models, too?" The answer is that hot rod models are the ultimate expression of that creative freedom. One astute observer puts it this way: "If you get a 1969 GTO kit, you can modify it and customize it, but it's still a GTO. With a hot rod kit, you can start with just a frame and design a whole new car as you go."

George Toteff, one of the creative forces behind both AMT and MPC, agrees. "Those hot rod kits," he says, "let kids put their energies into being creative, not just putting a body together."

The idea of putting a car together in one's own way has always been the major appeal to building a hot rod, whether it was a full-size car or a model. Revell and AMT both took that concept to a logical conclusion. Revell's "Custom Car Parts" and AMT's "Hot Rod Shop" car parts packs allowed creative modelers to pick and choose the parts to build a truly individual model.

Modelers could start with a frame pack, add suspension parts from a second pack, an engine from a third, and a set of wheels and tires from a fourth. Both companies even offered a choice of bodies ranging from T-buckets to Bantam roadsters to Fiat coupes.

"That was the best thing about the parts packs," says Jim Keeler of Revell. "You could build a complete model without even buying a kit!"

Hot rod models were a way for kids (and adults) to share in the love for cars that captured America after World War II. The model companies produced thousands of different kits, many of them based on contemporary hot rod and custom car trends.

This is a story about those model kits, about the companies that produced them, and about some of the people who influenced and designed them.

Although the hobby endured some rough times during the 1970s, model car building and collecting is bigger than ever. Some estimates place total sales of plastic model car kits at more than $1.5 *billion* annually.

As you're reading this, try turning on a tape recorder so you can play it back to see how many times you said, "Hey, I built one of *those!*"

Any kid in the '60s would have loved this workbench. On display are AMT's '25 *Double T* chopped coupe and Revell's *Stone-Woods-Cook* '41 Willys drag coupe. In the background are autographed photos from Tom Daniel and Don Emmons.

STONE–WOODS–COOK
'41 WILLYS
Revell
"T" Chopped Coupe
1925 Model "T"
DOUBLE "T" KIT
Build 2 Complete Cars
WHITEWALLS INCLUDED
amt
COMPETITION COUPE
Stone Woods Cookie

# chapter one

# AMT Corporation

*We could make a model of anything, stick it in a brown paper bag, and sell a million of 'em.*
—AMT sales executive, 1964

Late in 1944, American manufacturers began to realize that World War II might be near its end. In anticipation, they laid plans to convert to peacetime production as quickly as possible after the war.

When thousands of GIs returned home in 1945, one of the first things they wanted was a new car. Even by 1947, though, new cars were still scarce, as the companies struggled to revive their auto assembly lines. In many places, dealers might have only one or two vehicles to show to prospective customers.

In response to that shortage, West Gallogly, a Detroit attorney, came up with a great idea: Why not produce scale models of the new cars in all the available colors? That way, dealers short of cars could display the models to encourage orders.

After the war, the scrapping of wartime equipment provided an abundant, inexpensive supply of aluminum. Because it was cheap, easy to get, and relatively simple to use, Gallogly's staff cast the original models in aluminum. Consequently, he named the company Aluminum Model Toys.

The models were produced in 1/25 scale because it was an easy scale for engineers and pattern makers to use. Pattern bucks were sculpted at 1/10 actual size. During the tool-cutting stage, pattern makers used a pantograph to reduce the original form another 2 1/2 times, resulting in a model that was 1/25 actual size.

AMT's first two hot rod kits were the 1932 Ford "Deuce" coupe and roadster. The coupe offered a Chevy 283 V-8 with six carburetors, while the roadster was equipped with a Chrysler Hemi V-8. Cycle fenders and Moon wheel covers were options on both kits.

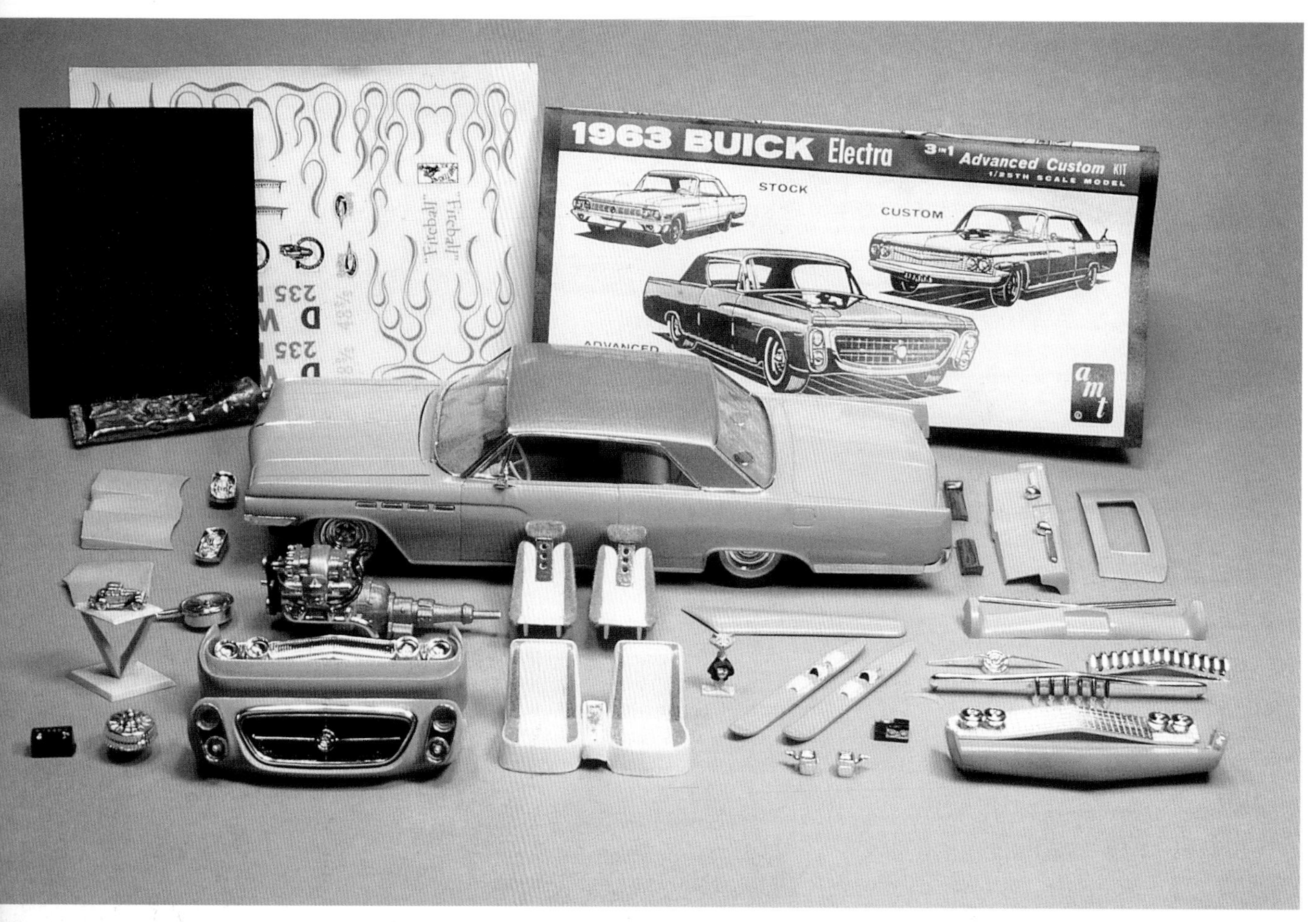


AMT 3-in-1 Customizing kits offered builders a choice of factory stock, custom, or racing versions. This 1963 Buick showcases many of the custom features available to model customizers: alternate front and rear treatments, engine and interior options, and great accessories such as water skis. *Rick Hanmore*

Gallogly already had contacts with Ford Motor Company, so by 1948 he introduced miniatures of the new 1948 Ford for dealer showrooms. The miniature Fords were an immediate hit with dealers, and orders for them began to mount. In many cases, dealers would give the models away to people who test-drove or purchased a new car. Thus, the miniatures became known as "promotional models."

Postwar technology advances soon allowed the company to switch from aluminum to plastic. Pattern maker George Toteff developed a system of cam-driven, sliding mold inserts that moved as the mold frame was opened and closed. The new molding process resulted in one-piece plastic bodywork for the models, rather than the awkward multipiece bodies that were required previously.

Toteff also worked with Dennis Eastman to develop appropriate plastics for the molding process. By 1949, they stopped using aluminum entirely. Since the company was no longer working in metal, Gallogly shortened the company name to just the initials—AMT—and a modeling legend was born.

Period-perfect custom touches on this 1940 Ford sedan include wide whitewalls on red wheels, cheater slicks, flames, and a corduroy interior. AMT's sedan kit offered modelers the choice of a 1939 or 1940 grill, along with the usual custom options. *Jerry Shoger*

AMT worked constantly to improve its products and began producing finished promotional models for many of the American auto manufacturers. Designers, engineers, and pattern makers increased the level of detail and added bright chrome-plated parts. By 1957, AMT models were a popular addition to many new car showrooms, and to the shelves of model collectors. They were popular with kids, too, because they offered a heavy-duty stamped metal chassis with heavy wire axles. Some even featured a friction motor.

Then, in early 1957, AMT designers came up with an intriguing concept. By boxing unassembled models and adding some extra "customizing" parts, AMT could sell the kits to hobby and toy stores, thus increasing its market significantly.

"Budd Anderson was actually the guy who came up with the kit idea," says long-time kit designer David Carlock. "He reasoned that we could sell our promotional models in a kit form, add additional detail and customizing parts, and sell them to hobby stores."

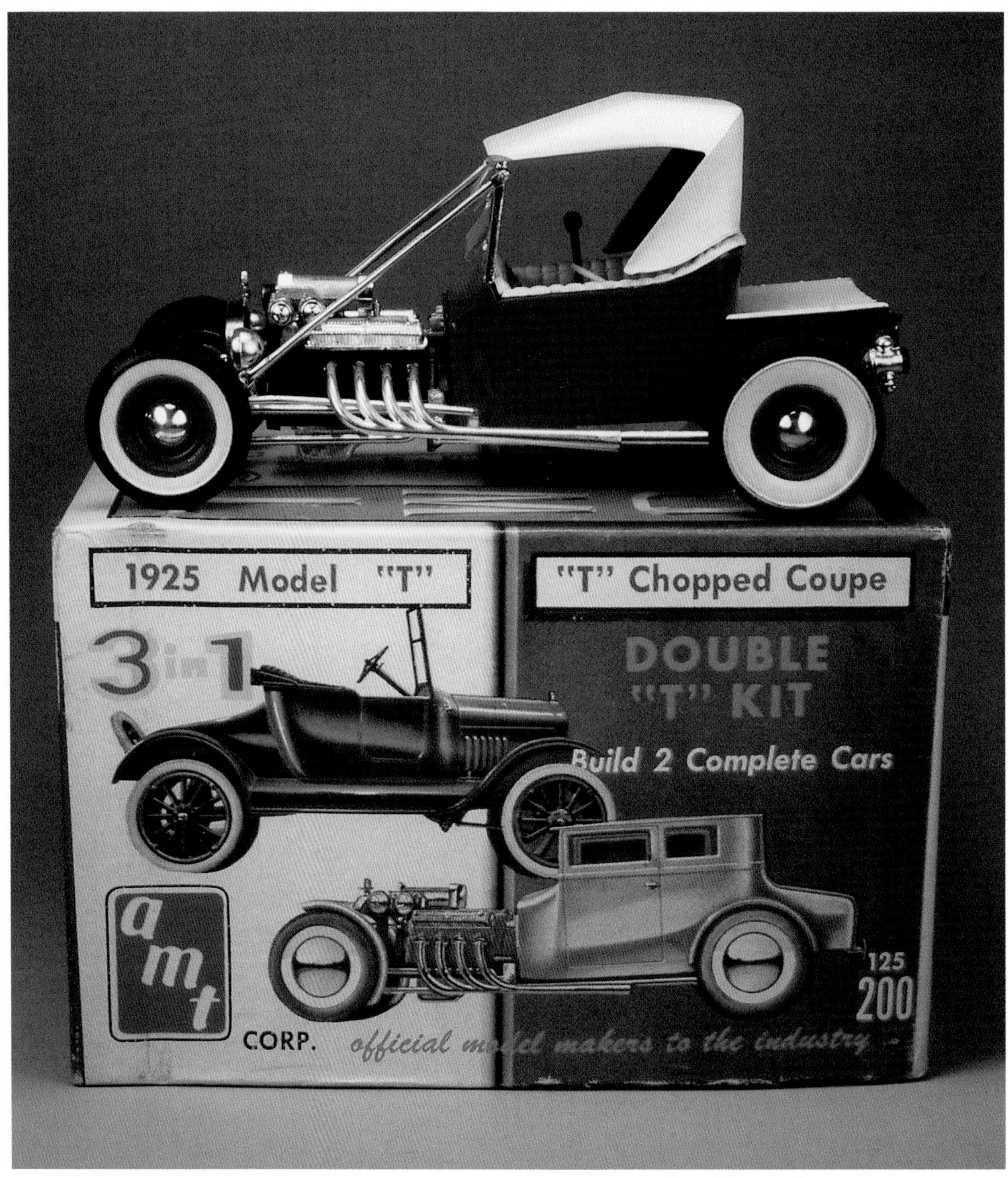


Double kits such as AMT's 1925 "Double T" provided two complete models in every box. Modelers could build a stock 1925 roadster or pickup, a chopped hot rod coupe, or a hot rod roadster with a choice of pickup box or turtle deck. *Rick Hanmore*

A number of manufacturers, including Revell, Aurora, and Lindberg, offered plastic model assembly kits, which were very popular with children. A wide range of kits included the fastest jet fighters, warships, birds, and even famous movie monsters like Frankenstein's monster and the Wolfman.

Those kits could only be built one way, though. AMT planners figured that kids in love with cars would go crazy for model car kits that encouraged them to "design" and build models of their own, so they released the models with a fistful of optional custom parts. Those parts allowed kids to build a model as a factory "stock" version, as a stylish custom, or as a race car.

AMT introduced its "3 in 1 Customizing Kits" early in 1958. By the time the kits were released, they included one-piece plastic chassis with relief details of the engine and suspension, along with a simple interior with a separate dashboard and steering wheel. In addition, modelers got fender skirts, louvers, spotlights, wild decals, and many popular contemporary custom touches.

The response was immediate. Kids (and adults) went crazy for the new kits. "I think it was the one-piece bodies," says George Toteff. "The kits gave the kids a kind of instant success, because they were easy to put together. The one-piece body had a lot to do with that. Plus, we added a 4x6-inch chrome shot with lots of custom parts." AMT's new "customizing kits" revolutionized the model building hobby and developed immediately into a major market segment. Full-size automotive magazines embraced the kits and published feature articles about them. Articles showed famous customizers like George Barris using model kits to test paint and styling ideas.

AMT followed with a strong product line for 1959, introducing many all-new models to reflect the styling changes coming from Detroit. New car kits like these were referred to as "annuals," because new kits were introduced every year to keep up with Detroit. In the meantime, though, designers began to look more closely at some of the model hot rods introduced by other companies. Most competitors' kits were simple, with one-piece chassis, minimal detail, and crude construction.

Many full-size car enthusiasts considered the 1932 Ford "Deuce" to be the quintessential hot rod,

AMT advertising included beautiful illustrations by staff artists Al Schrank, Kenny Wiktorowski, and art director Al Borst. This original 1961 artwork by Borst showcases the new 1936 Ford kit in both stock roadster and custom coupe configurations. *Dennis Doty*

# MODELING NOTES

*By Budd Anderson*

HEY, HOW ABOUT this. A brand new magazine on model cars. This is just great; my thanks to the swinging Petersen Publishing Company with the editor being an avid builder and collector himself, namely, Bill Neumann, and it's a pleasure to be a part of it.

First off, let me explain, I don't care to build the kind of models that look like they came from outer space. Instead, I style and build my models with the thought in mind

notice in photo #1, I cut my thumb. I've done that for years too, just like all model builders have at one time or another.

The car I'm building here is a '58 Chevy Impala hardtop, at least it started out this way. Then I got the bug to make a pickup out of it as I'm nuts about trucks anyway.

The cab and pickup bed came from a '64 Chevelle El Camino kit. I used the power tool in my hand equipped with a saw blade to cut away the rest of the body, and also to cut off the top and deck lid on the '58 Impala.

Next came the job of fitting the El

Photo #2 shows where I'm measuring off to insert the front wheel well opening from a Corvette. I didn't want such a slash-away wheel opening as on a stock '58, so I decided to hack up a 'Vette for parts. I'll do close to the same thing for the rear. By using the Corvette panel up front, I'll have two vents that will fade into the doors. Using the Corvette fender also allows me to tuck in the fenders, should I want a very radical front end.

The interior on this car will use the El Camino back panel with the '58 Impala floorboards and its wild custom dash.

## Budd Anderson: The Kat from AMT

Budd Anderson was a lifelong model builder who actually worked for Revell before he went to work for AMT.

"I was primarily a model maker or pattern maker," he said in an interview several years ago. "I worked for Revell in the mid-1950s doing patterns for model ship kits. I finally did get to work on a car model, though. That was the Pontiac Club de Mer."

From Revell, Budd moved to AMT. At first he worked in the model shop, but soon found his niche in public relations and sales. In the early 1960s as model car kit sales gained momentum, Budd began to write a monthly column for *Rod & Custom* magazine.

"Actually, it was just an ad," he recalled. "But we did it in that format so we could have a little fun with it. I talked about new AMT kits and ideas for building them. It was pretty popular with the kids."

In addition to his other duties, Budd traveled to car and hobby shows to showcase AMT models. "We were at a car show in New York or Chicago, some place like that. I was walking down the street with some people and this little kid pointed at me and said, 'Hey, there's that cat from AMT.' I liked the sound of that. At the time, Barris was spelling the word 'custom' with a K, so we changed it to Kat, and the name stuck."

Budd left AMT in 1964 and went to work for the Industro-Motive Corporation, where he helped develop nearly a dozen incredibly complicated model car kits, including the Bill "Maverick" Golden *Little Red Wagon* drag truck. In 1966, he moved to Model Products Corporation (MPC) and introduced a line of "Budd Anderson Master Kits." By 1970, he had moved into the automotive aftermarket, where he developed a number of products to customize full-sized cars.

He remained a model car builder and contributed occasionally to model magazines. In the early 1990s, Budd was even working on introducing a new line of model kits showcasing famous custom cars. Sadly, he died in 1994 before he was able to realize that project.

Another of AMT's famous double kits was the "Double Dragster." Modelers could build both a top fuel rail and a Fiat altered coupe. The monstrous engine in the dragster is actually an Allison V-12 from AMT's "Custom Shop" parts packs.

especially when builders stripped away the fenders and added new wheels and a hot overhead-valve V-8. AMT designers looked at the latest trends in full-sized cars and developed a whole new series of kits called the "Trophy Series."

"The formula was simple," says AMT designer John Mueller. "A Trophy Series kit had to be a model of a popular vintage car like a Deuce roadster or a 1940 Ford coupe, something the hot rodders were building.

"Then we added extra chrome parts. We budgeted so many square inches of chrome parts for each kit. Trophy Series kits got a lot more chrome, sometimes twice as many square inches of chrome parts.

"In fact," he says, "Trophy Series kits had more parts overall. They were the first AMT kits with engines, and they had detailed, multipiece chassis, along with custom parts to build different versions.

"And of course," he adds, "all the kits included a little show trophy of some kind."

AMT's first hot rod kits, released in 1959, were a 1932 Ford Roadster, a 1932 Ford five-window coupe, and an inboard runabout pleasure boat called the "Customizing Boat Kit." Each kit offered three different versions: factory stock,

AMT's 1957 Chevy Bel Air hardtop stayed in constant production for 36 years after it was introduced in 1962. The kit included a stock 283 V-8 or a blown 409 for the drag racing version. *Rick Hanmore*

street rod (a finned custom in the case of the boat), and competition (drag racing). In each case, clever engineering allowed modelers to "set" the parts together to review all the possibilities before deciding on a final version.

Boxes were unique to each kit, something new for AMT. The annual kits were offered in generic boxes that had a small label on the box end to identify the model inside. The 1932 Fords, though, got special colorful boxes with paintings of all model versions. The hot rod versions on the box tops were equipped with hot new V-8 engines, flame and scallop decals, whitewall tires, and flashy "Moon" hubcaps. Parts diagrams on the box sides showed the myriad of parts available to build every version of the kit.

Like the customizing kits before them, the 1959 Trophy Series kits were an immediate sensation with model car builders. "The Deuce kits really took off," says George Toteff. "We did the coupe first, and we were 11 months behind in filling orders. So we brought out the roadster and tried to fill the existing orders with that. But then the roadster sold out for almost a year! We sold a

Pickups were popular hot rods, and AMT's 1934 Ford was one of the best. The kit included an all-chrome 390 Ford V-8, and was designed so that modelers could build it with or without fenders in classic "highboy" style.

couple million of those kits the first year they were out."

Modelers clamored for more, and AMT was ready. For 1960, it added a 1940 Ford coupe and a sedan that could be built either as 1939 or 1940 versions. The two 1940 kits offered even more parts than before and included separate rear suspensions and axles, a first for AMT.

As exciting as those kits were to model builders, AMT had even more planned. Late in 1960 AMT released its first "Double Kit." The 1925 Ford Double Kit included parts for two models: a factory stock 1925 Ford Model T and a low-slung hot rod. By mixing and matching parts, modelers could build a stock T (either as a roadster with a turtle deck or as a pickup) and a chopped coupe with cycle fenders, an all-chrome suspension built from nearly a dozen parts, and a big Lincoln V-8. In addition, the hot rod offered a choice of multiple carburetion or a Latham supercharger. The box art showed nearly a dozen different versions that could be built with the parts in the kit.

That same year, AMT scored another coup when it signed California custom car builder George Barris as a consultant. By 1960, Barris had been producing full-sized custom cars for two decades and was recognized as one of the best designers and builders in the business. One of his cars, a fabulous custom 1929 Ford pickup called the *Ala Kart*, won the Sweepstakes trophy at the Oakland Roadster Show in both 1958 and 1959. Among other places, AMT trumpeted his affiliation with the company on the instruction sheet for its new 1936 Ford coupe/roadster kit in 1961:

> "With the introduction of the 1961 3-in-1 Customizing Kits, AMT Corporation is proud to announce the addition of Mr. George Barris to

our Design Engineering Staff. Serving as a Technical Advisor, Mr. Barris joins Chief Designer Phil Sheldon and Styling V.P. George Toteff to form scale model customizing's most progressive styling and design team.

"Mr. Barris comes to us from California, the original home of customizing, where he is known as the 'King of the Customizers.'"

In the same paragraph, AMT pointed out that all of its new customizing kits included "individually tailored parts and components." Tailored though the parts may have been, AMT engineers and designers made certain that they could interchange with other AMT kits, as well as with kits from other manufacturers. The result was a series of model kits that offered an infinite range of possibilities.

The popularity of the Trophy Series kits forced AMT to develop its own production lines. "Up until about 1961, we only had a couple of machines," says Toteff. "The bulk of our production was jobbed out to Eric Ericson of Detroit Plastic Products.

"But after the Deuce, we had to buy our own molding machines to keep up with the demand. We went from 2 machines to 15."

The early success encouraged AMT to develop a wide range of models during the following years. In fact, it engaged in extraordinary efforts to provide modelers with new products. Fourteen kit designers produced drawings for 35 model makers, who produced the patterns from which the mold tooling was cut.

"We worked 58 hours a week," remembers John Mueller. "We put in 10 hours a day Monday through Friday, and 8 hours on Saturday. At one point, we even started working on Sunday, too,

AMT released a 1953 Ford F-100 pickup kit in 1963, with custom parts designed by George Barris. The model shown is a replica of the *Wild Kat* Ford pickup, which was destroyed in a fire at the Barris Custom Shop in 1957.

The appeal of early Chevys in the drag gasser classes inspired AMT to release a pair of 1937 Chevys, a cabriolet and a coupe. Both kits came with a blown 427 and Cragar custom wheels.

Another popular gasser-class hot rod was the 1940 Willys. AMT's could be built as either a coupe or pickup version. Power came from a blown Olds with a B&M Hydro-stick transmission. AMT released the "Street Rods" series in the early 1970s.

AMT released dozens of kits that replicated famous drag cars. This is the 1967 top fuel dragster, *Wynn's Jammer,* by "Big Daddy" Don Garlits. The kit included a plastic base and a clear body to show off the interior components. *Bill Coulter*

but people couldn't remember what day it was after awhile.

"We really didn't mind. I didn't, anyway," Mueller says. "I went to work at AMT in 1962 just as the big hobby boom was gaining momentum, and it was fun from the beginning."

The designers and engineers at AMT were car people, Mueller explains. One, Dick Branstner, built a 1963 Dodge Super Stock sedan to do a little drag racing. Dave Carlock, then an AMT concept artist and designer, christened the car *Color Me Gone,* a name that became famous in drag racing circles.

"Dick brought the car to work one day," Carlock recalls. "We went out to the parking lot to look at it. I used some colored tape to put the name on the trunk of the car. It was a parody of a song that was popular at the time. Dick liked the name and it stuck."

Brantsner built several different versions of *Color Me Gone* over the next dozen years. Although AMT never did, both MPC and Lindberg eventually released models of his cars.

"Dick wasn't the only one building full-size cars," Mueller says. "A number of AMT employees worked on building their own full-size drag racing team for awhile. Budd Anderson had convinced AMT executives to buy Bill Cushenberry's famous 1940 Ford coupe, *El Matador,* to use at shows, and he came up with a Ford 289

In 1965, AMT advertisements urged modelers to get the "Big Three from TV." Two of those models were from the *Munsters* TV show. George Barris built the *Munsters' Coach* and *Dragula* from designs by Tom Daniel.

Cobra V-8 to replace the original engine in Cushenberry's car.

"We got a second engine at the time, too. There was this old barn across the street from AMT's factory. We got the use of that and cleaned it up to make a shop where we built our own race car, a little A/Altered T–bucket drag car. We even had our own tow truck, a 1955 Ford panel that we put together in our spare time."

Although company executives discouraged the drag team at the time, AMT went on to produce its own full-size cars.

"That was the Piranha," says hobby historian and writer Dennis Doty. "AMT opened a shop called AMT Speed & Custom in 1966 and built its own cars with body panels made of Cycolac, the same plastic it used to manufacture the models."

Customizer Gene Winfield ran AMT Speed & Custom at Phoenix, Arizona, and built six of the Chevy Corvair-powered Piranha coupes, as well as a drag racing roadster in 1967. AMT produced models of both the Piranha dragster and the coupe, which was marketed as *The Man From U.N.C.L.E. Car.*

The Speed and Custom shop didn't last long, though. "It was a lot of fun," says Dave Carlock, "but it wasn't profitable."

Drag racing was obviously an important aspect of full-size hot rodding, and it figured prominently in another breakthrough two-car kit. The "Double Dragster," introduced in 1962, included an AA/Fuel rail dragster and a Fiat gasser coupe. The kit featured a Scotty Fenn look-alike dragster chassis with an alternate frame for a twin-engine rail, as well as Chevy and Chrysler engines with multiple options. For the first time, AMT included decals for a current race car, a Fiat gas coupe called *Walt's Puffer.*

Throughout the 1960s, AMT continued to develop new concepts and ideas for model kits. It

# Don Emmons

Don Emmons is the guy who taught us all how to build models. He first gained national recognition when his 1/25-scale 1960 Corvette won best-in-show at the 1961 convention of the International Association of Automotive Modelers in Chicago. At a time when most "serious" hobbyists were scratchbuilding their models, Don used a stunning kit-based subject to take home the top award. His Corvette featured opening doors, poseable steering, and a candy apple red lacquer paint job.

Petersen Publishing covered the show in *Car Craft* magazine. When they discovered that Don was from their home base in California, they asked him if they could do a feature on the Corvette—"just like a real car," Emmons laughs. Bill Neumann, the new editor for *Rod & Custom* magazine, was so impressed with Don's work that he asked Don to produce a monthly how-to column called "Modelrama Q&A."

For the next five years, Don did his column and wrote dozens of feature articles for *Rod & Custom*, and for eight issues of *Rod & Custom Models*. Petersen installed a new editor in 1966 and discontinued model coverage, so Don moved over to *Model Car Science* magazine, where his "Detail for Real" how-to articles inspired even more modelers.

Don's work as a consultant for AMT lasted for 11 years, but in all that time the company released only one "official" Don Emmons kit. "The Alexander Brothers had done this beautiful show truck called the *Deora*," he explains. "AMT did a model in about 1965. A few years later, they redesigned the grill and some other parts and rereleased it as a convertible with my name on it."

When asked what part he took in redesigning the kit, Emmons laughs and says, "Nothing. AMT's design staff did it all. The marketing people just tacked my name and picture on the box and instructions. I really had nothing to do with it."

Don Emmons continues to work today as a freelance writer for such magazines as *Hot Rod*, *Rod & Custom*, and *Custom & Classic Trucks*. In the fall of 1998, he reintroduced his "Modelrama" column for *R&C* after a 32-year hiatus. The new column focuses on product reviews, trends such as diecast collecting, and features on various builders.

In 1996, Don Emmons was selected as a Hall of Fame award winner by the readers of *Scale Auto Enthusiast* magazine and the National Model Car Builders' Museum. "I'm just amazed by all this attention," he says about the award. "I never really thought I was doing anything that special. I just liked building models."

hired additional hot rod and custom styling consultants including Winfield, the Alexander Brothers from Detroit, Bill Cushenberry, and automotive writer Don Emmons.

Emmons was a model builder and a popular writer for *Rod & Custom* magazine. He worked as a consultant for AMT from 1962 until 1973. "I used to fly to AMT's factory about four times a year," he recalls. "I lived in Southern California, where many of the hottest new custom trends originated. My job was to go to car shows and races to photograph cars and features of cars. I'd send those back to AMT, and would follow up with the meetings to work with the designers.

"Walking into AMT's design room was like walking into an auto parts store," Emmons says. "They had Cragar wheels, Holley carburetors, injector stacks, and all kinds of new hot rod parts just lying around.

"The accessory parts companies, especially, worked to get their parts included in the kits. It was a big deal then to have one of your parts featured on the outside of an AMT kit box.

"The parts companies wanted kids to remember their products when the kids got to building full-size cars, so they provided examples to AMT and the other companies, who would produce miniatures of their parts for the kits. There was a lot more cooperation then."

The product line continued to grow. AMT began producing models of popular full-size hot rods and customs. Beginning in 1963 with the introduction of George Barris' famous *Ala Kart* pickup, AMT released dozens of different hot rod replicas. They ranged from rail dragsters by "Big Daddy" Don Garlits and Tommy Ivo to famous custom show cars like Bill Cushenberry's *Silhouette* and the Alexander

AMT has continued to release all-new model kits such as this 1951 Chevy Fleetline, part of a late 1970s series that also included a Bel Air hardtop and a convertible. The kit offered lots of possibilities. Compare the green "high school hot rod" on the left with the full-on leadsled.

In the 1990s, AMT's Blueprinter, Buyers' Choice, and Pro Shop series offered modelers the opportunity to buy newly released versions of kits that had been unavailable for years. Buyers' Choice kits like the Willys panel were rereleased with original box art and instruction sheets. At the same time, AMT released new hot rod kits such as its 1934 Ford five-window coupe.

Brothers' *Deora*, a custom pickup based on a 1965 Dodge A-100 pickup.

George Barris continued to develop projects for AMT, too. He produced pages of "Kustom Hints by George Barris" for AMT instruction sheets, and worked with them to manufacture models of his full-size cars as well.

In 1964 Barris built a wild hearselike Model T limousine for the ABC television show *The Munsters*. The *Munsters Coach* was so popular that AMT released a kit of the car later that year. For the second season of the show, Barris followed up with a wild dragster built from a coffin. The car, christened *Dragula*, was also produced as an AMT kit.

"Barris was really a showman," Mueller recalls. "But he was a great organizer and promoter, too.

"He came in twice a year to do his consulting work. George would sit down with our designers, go over proposals, and make suggestions about parts for the various kits. Then Dave Carlock and Dave Wilder would put together drawings based on his ideas."

AMT designers consulted with many well-known car people. John Mueller designed a number of dragster kits based on popular race cars. "I had a lot of fun there," he says. "I got to work with Don Garlits and Tommy Ivo on models of their cars. Getting to work with celebrities was a real plus."

Carlock believes that the popular subject matter was one reason for the success of AMT kits. The major reason, though, was always that the kits offered multiple versions. "It really helped the hobby grow, those multiversion kits."

George Toteff agrees. "One of the real keys was that 3-in-1 idea. Our research said that for every 10 kits we sold, we might actually have just three customers. Those people were buying the same kit over and over to build it different ways. That allowed kids to put their energies into being creative.

"And we were car people," he adds. "We didn't have marketing executives deciding what we produced. Our engineers and our designers got together and pitched ideas to the sales department. That's how we chose our kits."

Although Toteff left AMT to form his own company in 1963, AMT continued to produce hundreds of new kits through the 1970s. In 1978, AMT was purchased by Matchbox, the British toy manufacturer. Matchbox moved the operation to Baltimore, Maryland, where the company produced kits until 1982. At that time the Ertl Company, an Iowa manufacturer of farm toys and plastic model trucks, bought AMT and moved the company to Ertl's home base in Dyersville, Iowa.

From 1975 to 1989, AMT introduced few hot rod. The ones that were released were usually revised versions of earlier models. AMT did produce two 1934 Ford kits, a three-window coupe in 1975 and a two-door sedan in 1989. Both were panned by model builders because of poor fit and lack of fidelity to the original. The sedan was so poorly received that AMT has never rereleased it.

In 1996, AMT retooled the sedan kit and introduced an all-new 1934 Ford five-window coupe. The coupe combined the sedan chassis and running gear with an all-new body and fender unit. The kit was revised by designer John Mueller, who has a full-sized 1934 coupe in his garage. The model was much more accurate in shape and execution, and it allowed modelers to produce a full-fendered car or a fenderless highboy coupe. Two versions were offered—one stock coupe with vintage speed parts, and a street rod with a Heidt's-style independent front suspension and a Chevy V-8.

AMT's new 1934 Ford coupe has been well received in the hobby press and is considered one of the most accurate 1934 Ford kits ever done.

In the early 1990s, AMT initiated several programs that reintroduced vintage kits in small production runs. The first program was called the Blueprinter series, after AMT/Ertl's house magazine. Kits in that series included the original *Munsters Coach* and *Dragula*, the old "Double Dragster" kit, and an altered wheelbase 1966 Mustang funny car. Blueprinter kits were usually released in generic, heavy cardboard cartons with limited black and white graphics.

A second series, called Buyer's Choice, introduced other vintage kits with original box art. Among those was a 1933 Willys panel truck kit based on AMT's 1933 Willys gasser coupe and a series of dirt track race cars, among them a 1936 Plymouth coupe and a 1937 Chevy.

In 1998, AMT rereleased its original 1932 Ford roadster kit in a series called the Pro Shop. Pro Shop kits were another limited release series that was available only to hobby shop distributors. The 1932 roadster, originally introduced in 1959, has been released in many different versions over the last 40 years. This most recent release features parts from the kit's last release in the mid-1970s.

In the fall of 1999, AMT released an all-new 1932 Ford kit called the *Phantom Vicky*. Based on a design by West Coast automotive artist Jairus Watson, the kit features a convertible Victoria body mounted on an up-to-date street rod chassis. With more than 50 years of manufacturing experience, AMT continues to produce high-quality hot rod kits with the latest in speed equipment and design styles.

# chapter two

# Revell, Inc.

*It was like working in the biggest hobby shop you could imagine.*
—Jim Keeler, Director of Research and Development, 1961–64

Right after World War II, a British toy designer named Jack Gowland decided to move to the United States with his son, Kelvin. Kelvin Gowland had visited the United States during the war and felt that postwar America was a prime place to start a new business producing plastic toys.

At first Gowland & Gowland, as the company was known, manufactured pull toys with working features operated by cables and wires. Since they were unfamiliar with American marketing techniques, they formed a partnership with a California toy salesman named Lew Glaser to sell their products.

Glaser and his wife, Royel, had their own plastic company, which they called "Revell." According to former Revell executive Bob Paeth, Royel liked the name of the Revlon cosmetics line, and played with that to come up with the Revell name.

Reportedly, the Glasers convinced Jack Gowland to offer some of his toy cars as unassembled kits in a line of 1/32-scale models called "Highway Pioneers." Highway Pioneers kits are considered by many model historians to be the first all-plastic model car kits.

Although the original kit series concentrated on vintage and sports cars, Revell did produce a hot rod roadster in about 1955. This kit, manufactured in 1/32 scale, was a 1932 Ford done in

The *Outlaw* sold beyond Revell's wildest expectations. The decals in the original release were an incorrect lime green, as shown here. Later editions featured corrected blue-green decals to match the real car's actual colors. *William Bozgan*

In the mid-1950s, a hot rod was a 1932 Ford. Rodders stripped off the fenders, added larger tires at the rear, and dropped in a big V-8. Revell's first hot rod kit was this 1/32-scale *V-8 Hot Rod*, released in 1954.

contemporary fashion: chopped, channeled, fenderless, and equipped with a big V-8. It was part of Revell's "U.S. Modern Series." A mildly altered coupe version followed. They were the only hot rod kits that Revell would produce for another seven years.

Through the balance of the 1950s, Revell manufactured a number of different kits in scales ranging from 1/32 to 1/16. Primarily, it concentrated on 1/32 scale and released an entire series of current American car kits in that scale starting in 1955. The kits were well detailed even by current standards, but they were handicapped with a multipiece body that required patient assembly.

In one remarkable development, Revell teamed up with AMT in 1956 to market their car kits under a combined banner. AMT production manager George Toteff explains: "Both Revell and AMT used the same national sales firm to represent their kits. In fact, they displayed side by side in the firm's New York showroom.

"At some point, West Gallogly of AMT and Lew Glaser got together. Revell was already known as a top manufacturer of plastic kits," AMT's Toteff remembers, "but we had the automotive connections and recognition because of our promo line.

"West and Lew decided to produce a line of kits together. After a year or so, though, we started looking at doing our own kits in the larger 1/25 scale, the same as our promotional models, and the partnership dissolved."

While Lew Glaser was developing the deal with AMT, Royel Glaser began noticing popular

Revell released a series of customizing kits in 1957. Based on its 1/32-scale late model kits, this series included a 1956 Buick restyled by George Barris. This was the first time that Barris worked as a consultant for a model company. *Rick Hanmore*

California custom car trends. As director of Revell's Research and Development section, she was constantly watching new automotive trends. Using the talents of several well-known custom car builders, Revell released a series of customizing kits based on its 1/32-scale late-model car kits in 1956 and 1957.

Revell probably wouldn't have changed too much except for one development: AMT 3-in-1 customizing kits.

"Those kits just killed everybody," remembers Jim Keeler. "I'd been building Revell kits since the mid-1950s, but when AMT introduced those customizing kits in 1958, it wasn't evolution, it was *revolution*."

Jim Keeler started producing model contests in San Diego hobby shops when he was a teenager. As he realized how popular model cars were in California, he worked to get his contests included as part of area car shows. To get prizes, Keeler wrote to model companies. Revell's public relations chief, Henry Blankfort, sent kits. L.A.-based Petersen Publishing covered some of Keeler's model contests in *Rod & Custom*, and eventually Keeler developed regional contests all over southern California. He even promoted a national mail-in model car contest with the Tridents Car Show in Los Angeles—all of this before he graduated from high school!

"At the Winternationals Drag Races in 1959," Keeler says, "NHRA sponsored a car show and I convinced them to do a model contest there, too.

"The National Hot Rod Association was just taking off as a major national organization, so a lot people showed up. Revell and AMT were both there, and so was *Rod & Custom*. They did some coverage in the magazine, and that's how I got to know the people at Petersen Publishing. And of course, the model companies provided kits for prizes, so I got involved with them, too."

Revell
Authentic Kit

'56 Ford Pickup

A Revell first–
opening doors
and tailgate,
2 great engines

H-1283:198

Revell
Authentic Kit

MICKEY THOMPSON'S

CHALLENGER I

SPEED
RECORD
HOLDER

H-1281:200

The complex *Challenger I* tooling cost nearly double that of ordinary kits, but it sold well. At one point Revell considered manufacturing the kit with a clear body to show off the inner structure. Revell produced six of these models for shows; this is one of only two known to exist.

In 1961 Henry Blankfort called and invited Jim to Los Angeles to see Revell's factory in Venice.

"I went up because it was cheap," Keeler laughs. "My dad worked for Southwest Airlines, so I could fly to L.A. for a dollar." Blankfort met Keeler and took him on a tour of the plant. "It really was that proverbial well-oiled machine. I was pretty impressed."

During the tour, Blankfort took Keeler into the executive offices and introduced him to Royel and Lew Glaser.

They talked for awhile; then Royel Glaser gazed at Jim intently. Finally, she leaned forward and asked, "How would you like to go to work for us here?"

Though stunned, Keeler accepted. "I was 19 years old!" he says. "I don't think I needed the plane to fly home, I remember that!"

Keeler moved to Los Angeles a month later. "I didn't really know anybody in L.A. except car people, so I stayed with Ed Roth and his wife until I found an apartment."

Jim Keeler's first job at Revell was learning the production process. Working directly for Royel Glaser, he had the run of the factory. "I used to spend my lunch hours just wandering through the various shops, trying to learn everything."

Within the first few weeks, Keeler had developed ideas for new releases and was ready to present them to Revell's product selection committee. "I picked three," he says. "My idea was to counter AMT's 3-in-1 concept with kits introduced in groups of three—one race car, one street/custom car, and one Roth car."

Keeler had met Ed Roth when both were working at California car shows. "I really liked his cars. They were so fresh and different, and I thought that modelers would go for them."

Revell's first Roth car was the *Outlaw*, a T-bucket lookalike with a hand-formed fiberglass

Revell had to wait until 1962 to offer a response to AMT's Trophy Series kits. Revell's first releases were a 1956 Ford pickup, the *Outlaw* show car by Ed "Big Daddy" Roth, and Mickey Thompson's incredible *Challenger I* land speed record car.

From the beginning, Revell's hot rod models emphasized drag racing. The Stone-Woods-Cook 1941 Willys was one of the best-known A/GS coupes on the strip. Revell's kit featured opening doors, hood, and trunk, as well as poseable steering.

body. Companion vehicles in the release were a 1956 Ford F-100 pickup and Mickey Thompson's *Challenger I* land speed record car.

"I picked the Ford pickup because they were really popular on the streets, and because no one else was doing anything similar. And the *Challenger,*" he says, "I picked that because I was so impressed with Mickey and that car. I was a big fan of land speed record cars, and that one was really special. Those cars are kind of the ultimate hot rod."

*Challenger I* was a four-engined behemoth, which ran 401 miles per hour at Bonneville. The Revell model was an incredibly complex undertaking. "At the time," Keeler remembers, "it was one of the most expensive tools ever cut. It cost about $80,000 at a time when most tools cost between $25,000 and $40,000."

To offset costs, Revell used as many parts in common as possible. "I remember that we included four blown Pontiac engines in the *Challenger,* so they used that pattern as a second, custom engine in the Ford pickup, too."

Keeler had a wide range of responsibilities in addition to proposing kits. He wrote the product profiles, which outlined every aspect of the kit; produced a parts breakdown; and provided preliminary exploded-view drawings. After the kit was approved, he worked with the engineering department to obtain measurements and photos of the real car.

Once engineers created the drawings, the plans were sent to the model shop, where Revell's model makers carved masters, or "bucks." The finished bucks were used to create resin and epoxy patterns of each part, generally 1/10 of the actual size. Those patterns went to the machine shop, where machinists used pantograph machines to scale the parts down to 1/25 and cut them into the tool steel inserts for the mold frame or "shoe."

That tooling was refined and given detailed engraving. Then production engineers ran molten plastic through the tool to get a "test shot" of the plastic parts. "We used test shots to make certain that the parts were formed properly and they fit together," Keeler says. "If there was a problem, the engineers and machinists worked to correct it and we ran another shot."

As the tooling and production teams worked to complete the mold tool, artists and photographers developed instruction sheets and box art.

Bob Tindle was a member of Revell's *Show & Go Team*. His *Orange Crate* 1932 Ford sedan doubled as a drag car and a show car, and won trophies in both arenas. More than half of the parts for this kit were chrome-plated.

"Revell had some of the best artists in the industry, especially Jack Lynwood and John Steele," Keeler recalls. "They did all of the paintings for the box art, and we'd hang those in Revell's offices once they were finished with the art. It was pretty impressive."

Keeler also wrote instruction sheet copy. "I had a million things to do, keeping track of all those processes," he says. "And you have to remember that we might be working on a dozen different projects at once."

In fact, Keeler was so busy that he convinced Revell to hire another R&D specialist.

Bob Paeth was an Oakland, California, firefighter who had been promoting model contests in the San Francisco area while Keeler worked in southern California. Revell noticed him when he began working on a contest for the Oakland Roadster Show.

"I remember in January of 1961 I called Al Slonaker at the Oakland Roadster Show to ask about a model display," Paeth says. "I figured we'd get about 12 or 14 models."

Slonaker agreed and referred other inquiries to Paeth. "By the time the show started, we had a contest with about 60 models, and George Barris for a judge. I was amazed."

Like AMT, Revell released a series of "double kits." However, Revell's were nearly all drag cars. The first such kit was a pair of Tony Nancy's *22 Jr.* dragsters, released in 1964.

The next year, entries nearly doubled. AMT provided trophies and Barris judged the contest for a second time. After two years of sponsorship from AMT, Paeth decided to contact Revell for help. Along with Revell's assistance came Jim Keeler.

"I think we were getting ready to close up on Sunday night," Paeth says, "and Jim came up to the table. We talked for a few minutes, and finally he said, 'Would you like to go to work for Revell?'"

Paeth interviewed with management and went to work in May 1963, just as Revell was gearing up for its first national contest, the Revell/Pactra Model Car Nationals. Paeth shakes his head when he remembers. "Jeez, we had a lot to do. In addition to all the product development work, we had to administer this incredible contest.

"It was all by mail. People entered their models in local hobby shop contests. From there, all the winners were mailed in to Revell.

"We sent out about a half-million instruction sheets on stuff like packaging your model," Paeth recalls. "They didn't have all those little foam peanuts then, so we told people to pack their models in popcorn.

"We got some real strange stuff in the mail," he laughs. "One guy didn't realize you were supposed to *pop* the popcorn first, so he sent his model in unpopped popcorn, which completely destroyed it. Another guy sent his packed in buttered popcorn and it was so greasy we couldn't get hold of it!

"The best one, though," Paeth says, "was a guy who packed his model in caramel corn. We opened up the package, and it was this sticky, gooey glob

Custom Car Parts offered model builders 36 different packs with thousands of parts to modify other kits. And if you wanted, you could combine them to build complete cars. These five packs had enough parts to build a complete T-bucket hot rod with a 283 V-8.

with wheels. There was caramel corn and strings of caramel stuck all over it. What a mess!"

By the time all the entries showed up that first year, Revell employees unpacked almost 10,000 model cars. "We had this mound of popcorn in the warehouse where we were judging," remembers Jim Keeler. "It was about 25 feet high. Once I got up on a stairwell and jumped into it."

Keeler and Paeth went through the models for two straight days, picked the best ones, then invited celebrity judges Dean Moon and Ed Roth to judge the finalists.

"After that, we changed things a little," says Paeth. "The next year, the winners went to regional contests, and only the regional winners came to Revell."

Florida modeler Augie Hiscano remembers those contests well. In 1963, his *Black Bandit* super modified won the National Master Craftsman Award. Hiscano equipped the model with dozens of brass parts, including complete working throttle linkage, working steering, and a movable clutch.

In 1964, Hiscano built a roadster with parts from the Revell *Beatnik Bandit* and Jaguar XK-E

Revell produced six Ed "Big Daddy"Roth show cars between 1962 and 1966. The bubble-topped *Mysterion* at left featured two all-chrome Ford 406 V-8s. The *Surfite* was based on an English Austin chassis. Revell's kit included a surfer's tiki hut, too.

kits. Like his earlier model, the "XKR" roadster was detailed with handmade brass pieces.

"We remembered Augie's super mod from the year before," Paeth says. "When we unwrapped that roadster in 1964, we knew *exactly* who built it."

Hiscano and the other regional winners were flown to Los Angeles where they stayed at the Sheraton Marina hotel. "We were treated like royalty," he says. "They paid for my ticket, so I brought my wife with me. They had convertibles with chauffeurs for all the winners, and they took us all over."

Revell treated entrants to tours of the Roth and Barris custom shops, Disneyland, Seaworld, and Revell's plant. "We were even on TV," says Hiscano. "We also got to meet Revell's 'Show and Go Team' consultants—people like Tommy Ivo and Tony Nancy, and Roth, too. It was incredible."

By the time judging was over, the contest was a tie between Hiscano's roadster and a scratchbuilt semitruck built by Bob Nordberg. "They rented my model for a year," Hiscano recalls. "It was mounted in this big plastic bubble and they

Revell also worked with Big Daddy to release nearly two dozen Rat Fink and monster kits. This is *Drag Nut,* riding a Bantam altered roadster. Revell used regular car components for many of these kits, then added the special monster parts. *Drag Nut*'s eyes even glowed.

Gasser-class drag cars were a Revell favorite. These two are the Thames panel (l) and the 1951 Anglia. Both kits featured opening doors, hoods, and poseable steering. Tinted window glass was a standard feature.

used it to promote the company at shows. When I got it back, I got to keep the display, too."

As for Keeler and Paeth, they were still in charge of new product development. In addition to Tony Nancy dragsters and Roth show cars, they came up with an inspired idea. "All the extra parts we were putting into the kits were really popular," says Jim Keeler. "At one point we just thought, 'Why not sell just the parts?' We did some mock-ups with packages and showed them to our new products committee. They went for it right away."

Revell's Custom Car Parts packs were a sensation. "We did 36 different sets, from engines to speed equipment to car bodies to complete motorcycles," Keeler says. "You could use them to customize other kits, or you could put together three or four sets and build a model just from Car Parts. They sold like crazy."

After three successful years, Jim Keeler left Revell in mid-1964, leaving Paeth to carry on.

"I had fun," Paeth remembers. "I had a lot of ideas, and we actually got to do some of them."

One was a Thames drag panel. "I really liked those little gasser-class dragsters," he says. "We had already done the Stone-Woods-Cook Willys, and I wanted to do a Thames or an Anglia, but we couldn't find one. One day I was driving to work, and there was this little Thames panel truck parked in a driveway.

"I pulled up and asked about the truck, and the lady told me I'd have to talk with her son. Turned out the owner was Ken Berry, the actor who starred in *F Troop*!

"His truck was stock, but our engineers used it to design the body. Then we checked out a couple of other cars to develop the speed equipment."

Revell's 1975 release of Li'l John Buttera's 1926 T sedan was its first all-new hot rod replica in more than five years. Many hobbyists considered it to be one of the best kits of the decade, and it spawned several other versions.

Paeth had input to all aspects of product development. "One time," he says, "I wanted to do a 1956 Chevy two-door sedan but management had decided on a hardtop. I reasoned that we already had 1955 and 1957 Chevy hardtops, so a sedan was a natural.

"They weren't sure, but I finally convinced them to do it as a sedan. When we got to the box art, I noticed that all of the cars on our boxes were placed so that you saw a 3/4 view of the front. I decided that we should present the 1956 from the rear so it would stand out on store shelves a little."

Paeth also built models for product committee presentations. "In 1968 we were working on a proposed series of little Corvair-powered hot rods," he says. "I scratchbuilt this little C-cab truck we called *Patent Pending*, and presented it to management. They approved it and we used it as the basis for about a half-dozen kits, including a pickup called the *T-Bone Stake* and a little French taxicab called the *Meter Cheater*. What they didn't know is that I built the engine from an *AMT* kit!"

That Corvair-powered hot rod series included one kit called the *Amazing Moon Mixer*.

"We were goofing around in the office one day," Paeth says. "Lonnie Flanders, one of the engineers, discovered that our Apollo space capsule model would fit on the *T-Bone Stake* pickup bed. If you tilted it up, it looked just like the vessel on a cement mixer. We cobbled up some support parts, got it past management, and released it.

# History of the World According to Big Daddy

Y'see, when all the other model companies (like Monogram & AMT) wuz sellin' a lot'a *Ala Kart* kits, Revell wuz pokin' along sellin' model ships & other non–hot rod stuff, but the owner, Lew Glaser, had a wife, Royel, that was a go-getter. Like, she had boundless energy. She ran that Revell plant in Santa Monica with an iron hand. SHE was the one who called me and wanted to know if I was under contract to anyone! And at our first meeting, I suggested they hire Jim Keeler 'cause he was a model builder supreme (and a 16-year-old-kid I knew from the car shows). Jimmy started 'em on the road with the Car Parts series while they were frantically tryin' to make the molds for the *Outlaw*. Can ya picture a-16-year-old kid tellin' all those big-time model guys what to do? Well, he even bossed Royel around . . . but to their surprise, stuff started sellin' like hot cakes! Jimmy was a hero! It proved to me that what Von Dutch told me was true— "When you're GOOD, you're good YOUNG!"

Things were really cruisin' along for Revell. The artist was working on the picture for the *Outlaw* box, but I still didn't have a good nickname. I used Roth Studios 'til then, or just plain Ed Roth. But it was 1960, and I needed to come up with a good name for myself. So Henry Blankfort was the big idea man at Revell, and he sat me down in his office a day before the deadline on the box art was due at the printers, and he handed me a list o' names that I "oughta consider." I can remember "Spider" Roth and "Froggie" and some other not-so-tough names on that list of about 20 names. I didn't like any of them, so he started quizzin' me about my life, my family, and my friends, etc. I had five sons at the time. I was always over 250 pounds. At Bell High School, I was called "Big Ed." At about that same time (1961) in Santa Monica there wuz some wise guys startin' to recite poetry at these coffee houses, and when ya went to see 'em they'd serve some fancy coffees and listen to this really farout poetry. I never went, but I knew about 'em, but top it all off, the head poetry dudes were called "Big Daddy." So, when Henry Blankfort heard I had five sons, he immediately says like, Hey Ed, you're the biggest "Big Daddy" of them all. And that's how I got my new "Big Daddy" name on millions of Car and Rat Fink monster model kits. Gettin' a good nickname has been a secret of mine from the very get-go! Thanx to Henry Blankfort!

The goofy hats is a way other story. In order for me to get my kisser (face) on the boxes, Revell's idea (actually Royel's) was to take a bunch of pictures of me in my tuxedo. But I went down to the studio rentals place near Revell and rented me a bunch of studio props and costumes and I posed for pictures at Royel's swimming pool for a whole week. That poor photog, he was sweatin' and huffin' and puffin'. He musta gone thru 40 rolls of film. That Hasselblad o' his was smokin', but those pictures have been used on many model boxes.

Ya might be curious about them contracts I was always signin' and the deals we wuz makin'. There wuz so many of 'em because evertime I'd get another proposal I had to sign a contract, but I got cars and money and endorsements all over the place 'til 1964, when the Beatles came over. That wuz the beginning of the end of hot rodding as we knew it. Revell's sales went down and Lew Glaser died and so the company was sold to a Frenchman (about 1970) and then to Monogram (about 1980). In the late 1980s I signed another contract with Revell Monogram to rerelease the old monster kits and car kits and the *Beatnik Bandit II*.

*—Ed "Big Daddy" Roth*

"Big Daddy" Roth and Rat Fink name and device and *Beatnik Bandit* are trademarks of Ed Roth © 1999

Thirty years after he built the *Beatnik Bandit*, Ed "Big Daddy"Roth introduced a sequel. Revell was there, too, with an all-new kit that featured a miniature Rat Fink and a figure of Big Daddy—complete with white hair!

"It was just a lot of fun working there," he says.

Keeler agrees. "You know that film *Big* with Tom Hanks? Well, that's what it was like to work at Revell in the 1960s."

By 1969, both Keeler and Paeth were gone from Revell. Darrell Zipp (today of Zipper Motors, a manufacturer of fiberglass street rod bodies and parts) came in as R&D director. Under his guidance, Revell produced nearly 25 funny car and top fuel drag racing kits. Revell even began to sponsor teams, including the Don Schumacher's Vega funny car and Ed McCulloch's *Revellution* Dodge Demon funny car. Revell's funny car kits were highly detailed and complex. They spawned a whole new generation of builders who concentrated on intricate engine and chassis detailing, ranging from plug wires and fuel tubing to working butterflies in the blowers.

A French company called Ceji bought Revell in the mid 1970s. Ceji tried a number of different marketing strategies, including a low-cost line of kits under the Advent label. Advent kits were generally rereleases of earlier Revell kits. To save money and keep the retail price down, Advent dispensed with chrome plating on many kits. Others, like Ed Roth's original *Outlaw*, were modified

In recent years, Revell has rereleased many of its race car and Roth kits in the *Selected Subjects Program.* Modified rereleases include the 1934 Ford cabriolet (originally a Monogram kit). Since 1995 Revell has released a pair of 1937 Ford trucks, and all-new Deuce three-window coupe and roadster kits.

slightly from their original form and released under different names.

Then in 1975, Revell introduced an all-new hot rod kit that signaled a revitalization of the company. Li'l John Buttera, well known as a fabricator of drag racing chassis, built a trend-setting street rod based on a 1926 Ford sedan. Revell obtained rights to produce a model of the car.

Li'l John's 1926 T was an immediate success. With then-new chassis and suspension features and a 289 Cobra engine, the model was Revell's first all-new hot rod kit based on contemporary street styling and engineering in several years. Both Buttera and Revell followed up with touring car versions that were also well received. These kits inspired several new releases based on Buttera's chassis.

In 1984 Revell hired a new marketing director named Tom West, a kit designer and marketing specialist who had worked for both Aurora and MPC. West discovered that Revell still possessed many of the original molds of the kits that drove the company's success in the 1960s. Although many of them were scattered in pieces in Revell's warehouses, careful search and assembly revealed that most of the old hot rod kits were intact.

At the same time, West and Revell marketing executives negotiated a contract with Petersen Publishing to produce an all-new series of kits in conjunction with Petersen's venerable car magazine, *Hot Rod.*

"That really was the catalyst that turned things around," West says. "A lot of the kids who built Revell kits in the 1960s were now adults who had come back to the hobby. By tying in with *Hot Rod*, we were able to reintroduce all those old kits so the 'kids' could build them all over again.

"We changed and updated some kits like the 1957 Chevy, but we left a lot of the old race cars like *Challenger I* in original form. That series was a great success for Revell."

Revell went through more corporate buyouts in the 1980s and 1990s. An investment group called Odyssey Partners purchased the company along with Monogram Models, and moved Revell from California to Des Plaines, Illinois. In 1996, Binney & Smith, maker of Crayola Crayons, purchased both companies.

With heavy corporate backing, Revell began to rerelease even more of its old kits in a series called the Select Subjects Program (SSP). Kits such as the long discontinued *Miss Deal* 1953 Studebaker funny car again appeared in a hobby-shop-only program. Many of the early SSP kits sold out, a fact that encouraged Revell to search its tool banks for dozens of other vintage kits.

The big news from Revell, though, was the 1996 release of an all-new 1932 Ford three-window coupe street rod kit. Based on a car owned by Californian Rich Hart, the model featured an accurate three-window body, a fender and frame assembly that allowed for either a fendered car or a highboy, and up-to-date chassis components from Pete & Jakes' Hot Rod Parts. Revell followed up with a replica of Dan Fink's famous *Speedwagon* 1932 woody, and with a highboy roadster in 1997.

For the first time in nearly 40 years, modelers had a brand-new Deuce hot rod kit. They responded enthusiastically, buying the kit in big numbers.

Revell followed up with other vintage Fords, including a 1948 Ford convertible with flathead speed parts and a 1948 Ford woody station wagon released in 1998. Next in line was an all-new 1940 Ford convertible in the fall of 1999.

As a result of the mergers, longtime Monogram design director Roger Harney was instrumental in producing the new Revell vintage Ford and hot rod kits. "That 1940 convertible," he says, "is a model I've been waiting 30 years to produce."

Monogram
HOT ROD
All ★ Plastic
Acetate Parts Molded to Shape

# chapter three

# Monogram Models

*It's the only job I ever wanted.*
—Roger Harney, Monogram Design and Model Shop Supervisor, 1972–98

Robert Reder and Jack Besser started Monogram Models on the south side of Chicago right after World War II. Initially, they produced balsa airplane kits with a few plastic parts under the "Speedee-Bilt" label.

In 1946, Monogram Models released its first model car kit. The "Jet Racer" was a precut block of wood with plastic wheels and clear plastic windshield. It looked like a land speed record car, although no reference was made to that.

Monogram continued to manufacture wood and plastic models until 1954 when it introduced a midget dirt-track car in 1/16 scale. The "Midget Racer" was all plastic, and included a scale engine and driver figure.

Monogram followed with an all-plastic 1/24-scale Deuce roadster. The kit was a fenderless highboy equipped with a Ford flathead V-8. Molded in high-gloss blue, the Monogram "Hot Rod" set the tone for dozens of kits to follow.

Roger Harney went to work for Monogram Models in March 1957. His task as a model maker was to produce patterns for kit parts. He worked primarily in wood, but also with epoxy and polyester resins. "I remember the first thing I did for them was the stabilizers and floats for a Cessna float plane," he says. "Most of the time we

Monogram's second all-plastic kit was also its first hot rod model. The *Monogram Hot Rod* was produced in 1/24 scale and released in about 1955. The body and chassis were molded in halves to simplify tool-making.

Monogram followed up in 1958 with the *Drag Strip Hot Rod*, another 1932 Ford roadster. Plated parts were still in the future, so modelers resorted to bright silver paint to simulate chrome. Like the previous kit, the body was molded in vertical halves. *John Bowman*

worked in larger scales and then reduced the parts to actual kit size during the tooling stage, but on this project I had to do the patterns the same size as the final parts. They were pretty small, and tough to work on."

Harney's next job was to produce the body panels, grill, and seats for Monogram's "Sport Coupe," a low-slung 1932 Ford coupe. The model was manufactured in 1/20 scale and featured a clear sunroof, cycle fenders, and Chevy's new 283 V-8. "That was a neat kit," he recalls. "We tried to incorporate as many current features as we could, so the model was really up-to-date for the time."

Harney developed patterns for aircraft and missiles for the next 18 months, but late in 1958 he was moved into the design section. "That was fun," he says. "I designed the kit parts and breakdown, then I went out into the model shop and built my own pattern models.

"One of my early projects was what we called the 'Slingshot' dragster. It was actually a model of the Cook and Bedwell rail dragster. At that time, every car model we did was motorized, so I had to design the body to allow space for the batteries and electric motor. At the same time, I still had to maintain the slim shape of the dragster!"

The Deuce *Sport Coupe*, released in 1959, was slightly larger than Monogram's previous efforts, and was roughly 1/22 scale. Unlike the earlier flathead-powered roadsters, the coupe featured a new Chevy V-8, cycle fenders, and plated parts.

In 1959, *Hot Rod* magazine featured a new drag/show car built by Californian Jack Geraghty. The car, called the *Grasshopper*, featured a removable T-bucket body, which allowed Geraghty to race the car as a rail dragster.

"I was really excited by that car and thought we should do something like it," Harney says. "They didn't want to send me out to photograph and measure it, so we took the magazine article and developed the kit from that.

"We knew how big the engine had to be, for example, and figured out the other dimensions from there. It was all eyeball, mostly. It was nice because I didn't have to worry about putting an electric motor in it, so I could add a lot more detail to the suspension and chassis.

"I did the design, the parts breakdown, the parts layout, and all the body patterns for that kit. We called it the *Green Hornet*. We changed the wheels to match tires we already had in our inventory, and did some other changes, too. But it was the *Grasshopper*. If you look at the box art, that's even the same pose as the *Hot Rod* cover."

Harney's next project involved a series of vintage Fords. "We started working on some customizing kits, the first time we had done multiversion kits," he says. "I did design work and patterns for the 1930 Ford phaeton kit.

"AMT had already released its 3-in-1 Customizing Kits, so we went a little further and designed these as *six-way* kits."

Monogram's first dragster kit was the *Slingshot,* a rail patterned after the Cook & Bedwell car, which campaigned at drag strips in the Midwest. The envelope body contained provisions for batteries and an electric motor. *Rick Hanmore*

Monogram's "Build It Your Way" series included a 1930 Ford phaeton, a 1930 Ford cabriolet, a 1934 Ford three-window coupe, and a 1936 Ford three-window coupe. "We did the kits with a choice of coupe or convertible tops," Harney says. "Then we added custom and racing parts. That way you could build the coupes three different ways, or a cabriolet or roadster three different ways."

Monogram's second generation of hot rod kits eventually included a 1930 cabriolet, a 1930 Ford station wagon or "woody," and a 1929 Ford pickup. "Those were nice kits," Harney remembers. "We put in extra parts like surfboards and scuba gear, too. They were a lot of fun to do. One thing we did was make sure that the stock parts from the phaeton or cabriolet kits would fit them, too, so you could build stock versions of the woody and the pickup."

In 1961 Monogram released a 1/8-scale model of a Chevrolet 283 V-8. The kit was designed to produce many different versions of Chevy's hot V-8, including factory stock, street rod, and several different types of racing. The engine featured two different supercharger configurations, seven carburetors, and three different exhaust systems. With 135 parts in four colors, the kit was well received . . . but there was a problem.

"People kept writing and asking what to put it in," Harney recalls. "Nobody produced a model car that big, so all you had was the engine. We thought it was pretty impressive the way it was, but modelers wanted a car, too.

"I was involved with full-sized hot rods at the time and followed all the magazines," he says. "At that time, T-buckets were really gaining in

One of Monogram's best early kits was the intricate *Sizzler* dragster. The model offered many options, including a Bantam coupe body. Clear parts simulated the delicate wire wheels popular on early dragsters. *Dennis Doty*

popularity. Norm Grabowski had built his *Kookie T* that was on *77 Sunset Strip*, and Tommy Ivo had built a beautiful T roadster.

"I went to Jack Besser and Bob Reder and convinced them that we needed to do a car to put the engine in. The T-buckets with fiberglass bodies were pretty simple and straightforward, so that's what we did."

Monogram's 1/8-scale T was not a model of an actual car. In fact, many of the components were based on patterns produced for smaller kits. "We enlarged a lot of parts from the 1930 Model A kit," he says, "but I did all new patterns for the body, interior and top, pickup bed, and the grill shell."

Harney also scratchbuilt a 1/8-scale T model for the national hobby show that year. "A lot of it was wood and epoxy," he says, "but it looked good and it got us a lot of attention."

Monogram's *Big T* was an immediate success, and orders for the kit began to pour in.

In the midst of all that activity, Besser and Reder decided to move the factory. "They moved the whole thing to Morton Grove, Illinois, where we are today," Harney says. "At the same time we were trying to do all of our design and pattern work, we had to box it all up and move it!"

Monogram also hired a new custom car consultant during that period. "AMT had picked up George Barris, and Revell had Ed Roth," Harney recalls. "We wanted someone who was from the Midwest, though, who was still a big name in custom cars. So we approached Darryl Starbird. That was about 1961."

Starbird, like Roth and Barris, was one of the best-known names in custom car building. From his Star Kustom Shop in Wichita, Kansas, he produced top-quality custom cars that were taking trophies at car shows all over the country.

"Darryl would come in and work with our designers a couple of times a year," Harney recalls.

Creative model builders in the 1960s produced wild rods and customs. This one is based on Monogram's 1930 Ford phaeton, originally released in 1961. The candy lime green touring car was featured in *Car Model* magazine in the early 1960s. *Dennis Doty*

"He would check over the projects we were doing, and make suggestions about custom parts, wheels, engine accessories, all kinds of things. Then we'd work those over and add them to the kits."

Starbird was famous for building cars with clear bubble tops, so that feature was incorporated into several new Monogram kits. "I think both the 1955 Chevy and the 1958 T-Bird had bubble tops," Harney says. "I remember that the top on the T-Bird was tapered and really graceful.

"Once we started doing models of Darryl's showcars, a lot of those had bubble tops, too."

In a reversal of the usual process, Monogram hired Starbird to build a full-sized version of the *Big T* for shows. Harney remembers worrying about the car. "We had done the *Big T* essentially by eyeballing it. We didn't have an actual car to measure or photograph, so I was concerned about how the full-sized car based on our model would turn out. But he did a good job and the car was pretty nice. I never got to drive it, though."

Monogram showed the real *Big T* at NHRA's Indy Nationals in Indianapolis in 1963. "Every time we showed that car, our sales for the kit would jump. People saw the car and ran out and bought a model," Harney says. "It was a great promotion." Monogram later released three different versions of the *Big T*: The *Big Drag*, *Big Rod*, and *Big Tub*.

While Monogram was at Indy, company president Jack Besser saw another car that impressed him. Larry Farber's *Li'l Coffin* show car was a radically modified 1932 Ford sedan. Originally built by Dave Stuckey, a Starbird employee, the car featured a chopped cantilever top, which was supported only at the rear. "It was really a wild car," Harney recalls. "Jack liked it so much he bought it. Naturally, we did a model of it right away."

Monogram followed up its successful *Big T* series with a 1/8-scale 1932 Ford roadster, the *Big Deuce*, but sales on the Deuce were disappointing. "I think it was the extra five bucks you had to pay for it," Harney says. "It was more complicated, so naturally it was more expensive. I believe that we crossed some threshold somewhere, and people just balked at the price.

"It was at least as nice a kit as the Ts, but for some reason it just didn't sell like those T kits did."

Monogram's second generation of hot rod kits included several variations on the Model A Ford chassis. These three (from left) are the *Red Chariot* 1930 phaeton, the 1930 Ford "Woody" station wagon, and the 1929 *Blue Beetle* pickup.

Monogram continued to release models of Starbird customs, including the *Predicta*, a heavily modified 1957 Thunderbird, and the *Orange Hauler*, a custom Chevy pickup. "At least I think it was a Chevy pickup," Harney recalls. "He changed that so much you couldn't tell what it was. It was another wild car."

Monogram bought the *Orange Hauler* and gave it away in a national promotion in 1965. "I think some kid from Oklahoma won it," Harney says. "It was a big deal. Darryl delivered it personally. We got a lot of press from that contest."

Another Starbird car that Monogram bought was the *Futurista*, a three-wheeled show car with another of Starbird's trademark bubble tops. "We had Darryl build that one for us. Jack really liked his cars, so they put together a deal to build one just for Monogram. And again, it was done as a model."

By 1964 slot car racing was a growing and wildly popular aspect of the model car hobby. Monogram's planners looked at the market and began to invest heavily in slot car kits, many of them based on existing kits. "The problem with that, though," says Harney, "is that as soon as we got something out on the market, it was obsolete. That part of the market got really big in a hurry, but then it died out almost as fast.

"We went into it too heavily, and too quickly. When it died, we were left sitting with all this inventory, and that hurt us. In fact, we stopped doing new car models altogether and started to concentrate on the military stuff.

"We did a number of good armor and aircraft kits. With the escalation in Viet Nam, we repackaged a lot of those with that emphasis, and that sustained us for several years."

In 1961, Darryl Starbird signed on as a consultant for Monogram, which released several of Starbird's custom cars in model form. Like most of Monogram's models, the *Orange Hauler* was molded in color so modelers could build the kit without painting.

In 1968, Monogram planners came up with an idea for a hot rod based on a Mack truck. "I went to Bob Reder and told him about this concept for a hot rod beer wagon," says Harney. "But I had been reading about this guy in California who was doing designs for *Rod & Custom* and *Hot Rod*. He had done some drawings using our kits as a basis, and they looked really sharp.

"I told Bob that I thought we should see what the guy could come up with."

The California artist was Tom Daniel. Daniel had been producing drawings for Petersen Publishing since 1958, using the column title "Off the Sketchpad." When Petersen introduced a model magazine called *Rod & Custom Models*, Daniel added drawings based on popular new model car kits. His "Off the Model Sketchpad" renderings were popular with modelers and car enthusiasts alike.

Harney contacted him and explained the project. Daniel worked out some ideas and sent in three-view drawings of a Mack truck flatbed called the *Beer Wagon*.

"I remember when I got that concept, I looked at it and realized that it was going to be a *huge* model," Daniel recalls. "Even those older Mack trucks were pretty big. So I called them and they said, 'Well, scale it down a little.' So I reduced all the dimensions for the final design." In addition to the concept drawings, Daniel also did the box art for the finished model.

Monogram's 1/8-scale *Big T* was a major development in 1962. It generated big sales, too, even though at $10.98 it cost five times more than most 1/25-scale models. Monogram followed up with three new versions of the 1/8-scale T. The *Big Drag* used the blower and other parts from Monogram's earlier 1/8-scale Chevy engine kit. The *Big Rod* kit included American Racing Torq-Thrust mag wheels and a cylindrical gas tank in place of the pickup box. The *Big Tub* featured an all new phaeton body, top, and interior.

Another of Monogram's great hot rod kits was the 1936 Ford coupe. Unlike many other model hot rods during the period, this model retained the original flathead V-8, but equipped the engine with contemporary speed parts. *Mark Gustavson*

The *Beer Wagon* was the beginning of a successful partnership for both Monogram and Tom Daniel. But in the middle of that project, Monogram was sold.

"Mattel came east in 1968 and bought the company," says Harney. "They were doing huge business with their Hot Wheels toys and decided to get into plastic kits as well.

"Once the purchase was completed, they came in with all kinds of goofy stuff like Snoopy kits," he recalls. "That only lasted a short time, though, and they let us go back to doing what we thought was best."

What Monogram thought was best was a long series of Tom Daniel kits. "The market had changed," Harney says. "The kids who had started building kits in the 1950s and early 1960s were growing up. They were interested in other things, but there was a whole new generation of kids coming up behind them. We kind of geared the Tom Daniel stuff toward the younger ones."

From 1968 until 1975, Monogram produced 75 different Tom Daniel kits. Most of them were original designs, but some were revisions of existing Monogram kits such as the 1929 Ford pickup. According to Harney, "Tom worked as a consultant on our kits just like Darryl Starbird. He would introduce new parts like wheels and carburetor set-ups, and we would change the kits to match those designs.

"Primarily, though, we were doing Tom's original designs."

Daniel's second kit for Monogram had an unusual inspiration and became a huge sales success. "The surfers in California were wearing chrome-plated World War I German helmets, and calling them 'surfer helmets.'" Daniel says.

"I was looking at one of those and thought that it would fit just right on a T-bucket body, so I went home and did some sketches. In keeping with the World War I theme, I wanted to put an old Mercedes-Benz aircraft engine in the car. I

One of the earliest "funny cars" was George Hurst's *Hairy Olds*. Powered by two huge Toronado engine/transaxle combos, the wild 1966 Olds Cutlass delighted crowds with smoky four-wheel burnouts. Monogram produced a model of the car in 1967. *Bill Coulter*

found one in a museum, but it was just enormous, so I scaled it down. I added machine guns and some other stuff, too.

"At the time, there was this song on the radio about Snoopy and the Red Baron, and I thought that would be a great name for the car, so that's what we called it."

Daniel's *Red Baron* caught on immediately and became so popular that Bob Larivee of Promotions Incorporated obtained permission to do a full-sized version for car shows. The kit was one of Monogram's best sellers of all time.

"I went back for a consultation in 1972," Daniel recalls. "When I got there, they had this little ceremony and they gave me a built *Red Baron* model all plated in gold. Turned out that the kit had sold more than two million units by then. They were pretty happy about it."

According to Harney, Monogram kit designer Ken Merker was partly responsible for the success of the Daniel kits. "Tom would send us great drawings, including section drawings. But once we got those, Ken was responsible for the final forms.

"In addition to putting them into 3D, he also had to come up with engines and suspension parts to put under the models," Harney says. "Most of the drawings didn't show those parts, so Ken had to develop those on his own.

"His work on those kits was pretty special. They were easy to build. He did good designs, well thought out."

Customers agreed. "When I was a kid, those were the neat ones to me," says collector Curtis Hutton. "They were so different from what the other companies were doing. The box art was great, too. I built every one I could.

# Tom Daniel

Tom Daniel was an industrial design student at L.A.'s Art Center College of Design. In 1958, his final year of study, he was approached by Lynn Wineland, then editor of *Rod & Custom* magazine. Wineland wanted to know whether Tom would be interested in doing some artwork for the magazine.

"Lynn was actually the person who developed the 'Sketchpad' concept for the car magazines," Daniel remembers. "He even did a couple of the early articles himself.

"He had seen my work somewhere and thought my concept designs were pretty good, so he offered me a job doing concept cars and other artwork for the magazine. It didn't pay great, but it sure helped with my expenses at school!"

After graduation, Daniel moved to Detroit, where he worked in the design division at General Motors. "Mostly you worked designing parts of cars. Very few people did an entire car," he says. "The one component I remember best was the hood for the '62–'66 Chevy and GMC pickups."

Daniel moved back to California in 1965 and went to work for North American Aviation. "I worked on the Apollo space craft, doing component designs."

He continued to work for Petersen Publishing, as well, doing his "On the Sketchpad" articles and other art. It was work for *Rod & Custom Models* that caught Roger Harney's attention.

Daniel was involved in many other projects beyond his work for Monogram. He designed a supersonic rocket car for land speed record holder Gary Gabelich. "We really thought that the car, called the *Rocketman*, could beat the speed of sound. But Gary was killed in a motorcycle accident and the project died with him."

In recent years, Daniel has stayed busy with a wide variety of projects. An avid model railroader, he designed a series of scenic backdrops for his own company, HO West, and produced a series of laser-cut miniature buildings for Model Expo. In addition, he did concept designs for Peterbilt. "If you see any of their droop-snoot trucks, I'm in there somewhere," he says.

Currently, Daniel has done some new drawings for Monogram and has developed a series of cards and prints with subjects ranging from steam locomotives to updates of his original car designs.

"I liked doing those designs for Monogram," he says. "Their model kits were so well done. Monogram has always been first class."

Monogram did a series of smaller kits called the Forty-Niners. Most cars in the series, including this Fiat altered coupe, were produced in 1/32 scale. The drag cars in the series were beautifully detailed, especially when you consider that they cost less than half a buck! *Bill Coulter*

"They were molded in colors, so all you had to do was paint the details. When you're 12 that's important. Those kits just went together so well."

Phil Davis, who started the Tom Daniel Fan Club, was another avid customer. "I was a kid building models in the 1970s. Tom's theme cars were so exciting. I really think he started the whole weird show car movement in that era.

"And Monogram's kits were just great to build. You didn't have to fit the parts or trim anything. They just fell together. I tried to collect *all* of them. I remember that I could hardly wait to go to the hobby shop and see what was new."

"We always had good luck with those concept and show cars," says Roger Harney. "Whether it was the *Predicta* or the *Red Baron*, they sold well for us."

Roger Harney is still with Monogram as this is written. In 1972, he was promoted to supervisor for the design studio and model shop. In 1998, he was appointed director for Research and Development. "I've been here almost 45 years," he says. "It's the only job I ever wanted."

Monogram entered a completely new era when it hired California artist and designer Tom Daniel to introduce a new line of show cars in 1968. This grouping includes (clockwise from top left) the *Pie Wagon, Dog Catcher, Horn Toad, Rommel's Rod, Paddy Wagon, Tijuana Taxi, Red Baron,* and *Beer Wagon. Collection of Tom Daniel*

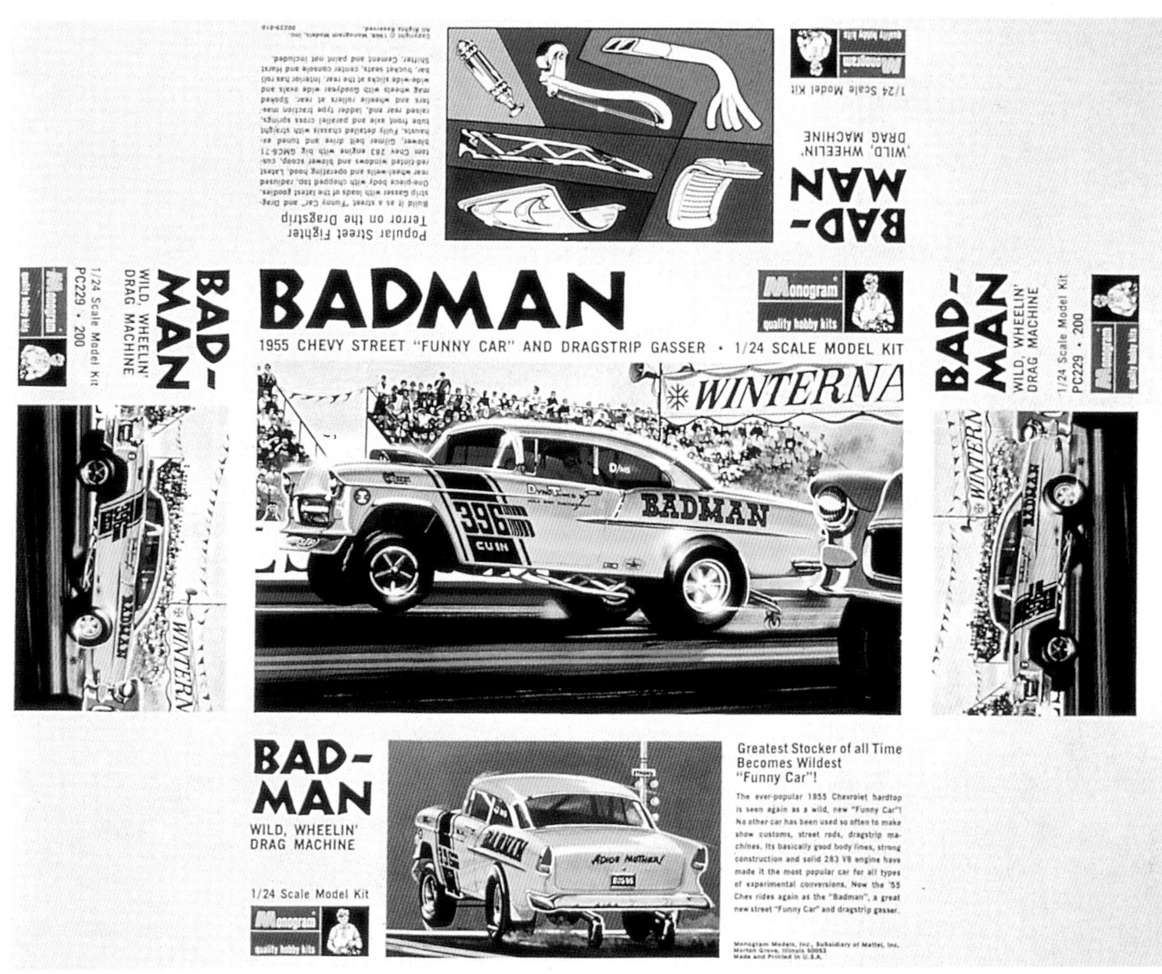


Daniel produced renderings for box art in addition to his work on concept designs. This layout is for Monogram's *Badman* 1955 Chevy kit. Note that the artwork is shown in finished location on five panels. *Collection of Tom Daniel*

Like all of the model manufacturers, Monogram went through some changes in the mid-1970s. Mattel sold the company to an investment group headed by Tom Gannon in 1975, and Monogram moved away from the Tom Daniel kits and many of their show car models.

In their place, Monogram introduced a series of mid-1950s Chevy kits: a 1953 Bel Air hardtop, a 1956 Bel Air hardtop, a 1957 Nomad wagon, and a 1957 Bel Air. Those kits suffered from awkward proportioning and were not well received. Monogram tried again with a series of Chrysler Corporation and GM muscle cars and was more successful.

In 1982, Monogram announced a series of NASCAR stock cars, followed by Camaro and Thunderbird pro stock kits in 1984. That two-year period is considered by many model builders to be the start of Monogram's turnaround. The stock car series was a huge success and spawned more than 100 kits.

For hot rod modelers, the major news from Monogram during the early 1980s was a pair of prewar Chevys. Monogram's 1939 Chevy coupe

In the late 1970s, Monogram released a pair of 1939 Chevy hot rod kits: a coupe and this sedan delivery. Although the Chevys were introduced as street rods, the kits were often used to build vintage low riders. *Jerry Shoger*

and sedan delivery kits featured big block Chevy engines. Both kits were first-time offerings and proved popular with model builders. Corporate design policy at the time was to offer detailed assemblies, but to combine as many parts as possible. Consequently, the kits included nice detail, but were simple to put together.

In 1987, Monogram offered another first. The new kit was a 1937 Ford slantback two-door sedan. With an up-to-date small-block Chevy, billet wheels, and other contemporary details, the 1937 Ford was another kit that never had been modeled before. Four years later, Monogram followed up with a cabriolet version that featured an even newer suspension set-up, a Carson-style top, and a custom Mullins trailer.

Along with Revell, Monogram was purchased by Odyssey Partners in about 1986. The two companies were combined, although their product lines remained separate. In its usual fashion, Monogram continued to turn out new model car kits in 1/24 scale (a European modeling standard) instead of the American industry standard of 1/25, a scale that was derived from pattern-making techniques. As the two companies integrated design and engineering efforts, though, that began to change, until the two companies were combined under one name—Revell-Monogram—in 1994.

In the 1990s, one of the major developments for both Revell and Monogram was the reintroduction of dozens of vintage kits in limited-run series. In Monogram's case, more than 20 of the original Tom Daniel kits were released in the Selected Subjects program. Other vintage kits included the mid-1970s Early Iron series of hot rod kits, including the 1930 Ford phaeton and woody, the 1936 Ford cabriolet, and the 1940 Ford pickup. Monogram even dusted off its 1959 *Drag Strip Hot Rod* and the 1960 *Green Hornet* T-bucket kits.

In 1996, Monogram introduced some new versions of early Daniel kits, including the *Red Baron* (packed in a tin collector's box) and the 1968 *Paddy Wagon* kit. For the new release, Monogram added a pair of prepainted comic police officer figures cold cast in resin.

"When I designed the *Paddy Wagon* in 1968," says Tom Daniel, "I wanted to include those two 'Keystone Cops' figures, but Monogram said no. So when we were getting ready for

In 1984, Monogram modified its 1934 Ford coupe kit into Billy Gibbons' *ZZ Top* coupe. Like Revell, Monogram has also released a significant number of vintage models in original form, including many of the original Tom Daniel kits. New hot rod kits included the 1937 Ford sedan.

the 30th anniversary of those kits, I tried again. This time they agreed, so I included them in the all-new box art."

To the dismay of many model builders and collectors, Revell-Monogram announced in 1999 that it was dropping the Monogram brand name for new kits, after 53 years of production. According to the press release, market research showed that the Revell name was more recognizable, especially in overseas markets.

"That's a shame," says longtime builder and hobby writer Bill Coulter. "Of all the companies, Monogram kits looked best when you opened the box. I loved the way their stuff looked. They were so well finished you almost didn't have to paint them.

"I'll miss seeing new Monogram model kits."

FROM THE HIT FILM/DU CÉLÈBRE FILM
More American
JOHN MILNER'S
Yellow Deuce Coupe
MORE AMERICAN GRAFFITI
FOR AGES 10 TO ADULT
ENFANTS À PARTIR DE 10 ANS ET ADULTES
1/25 SCALE MODEL KIT - MODÈLE RÉDUIT
RETOUCHED PHOTO OF ACTUAL CAR
PHOTO RETOUCHÉE DE LA VRAIE VOITURE
More American Graffiti

# chapter four

## Model Products Corporation

*We changed the way model kits were done. At MPC, we were much more sophisticated.*
—Dave Carlock, concept and kit designer, AMT/MPC/Ertl, 1964–1995

George Toteff, AMT's vice president for product design, made a critical decision in 1963. He decided to leave the company and form his own.

"I'd been with AMT for more than 15 years," Toteff remembers. "In fact, I was their first employee."

However, some business decisions by AMT executives didn't sit well with Toteff, so he made plans to move into other ventures. His departure was friendly though, and he stayed in contact with AMT president West Gallogly and others in the company.

"The first thing we did was to put together a tool-making company in Windsor, Ontario, near Detroit," he says. "I worked with Fred Binder to start that so we could cut tooling on a freelance basis for all the companies. And we formed our own company, called Model Products Corporation.

"One of the reasons we started up in Canada was that we could work two shifts," says Toteff. "That allowed us to come in well ahead of deadlines. It was a real advantage at the time.

"I had an agreement with AMT that allowed them first right of refusal on any new tooling that

One of most famous hot rods of all time was John Milner's Deuce coupe from the *American Graffiti* films. MPC reworked their Switchers 1932 Ford coupe kit to produce this model of the yellow coupe. *John Bowman*

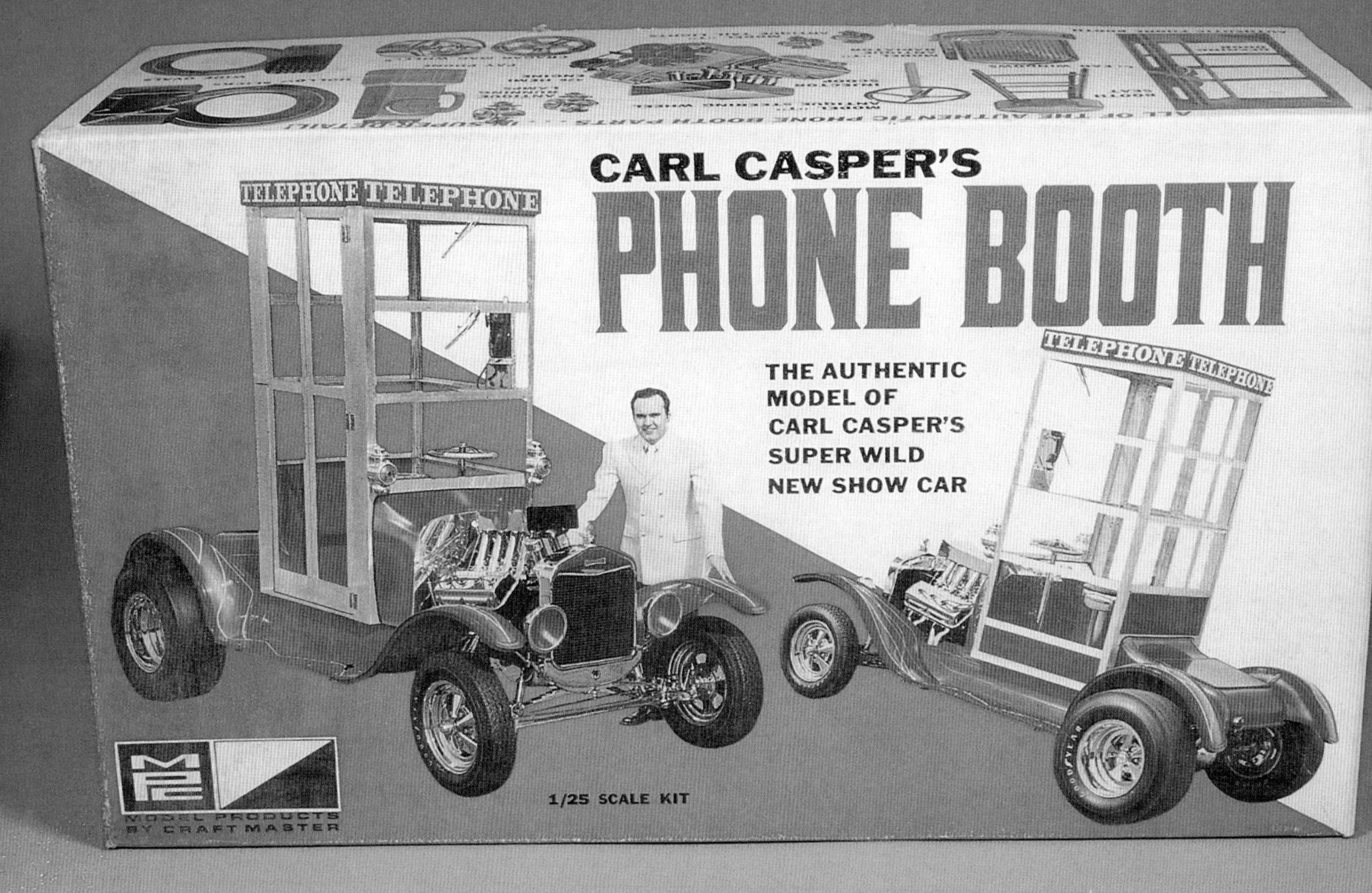


MPC worked with some of the top custom car builders in the country to produce kits. One of their earliest hot rod kits was Carl Casper's *Phone Booth T* show car, which featured a complete phone booth mounted to a T hot rod chassis. *Bill Coulter*

we did ourselves. It wasn't a noncompetition clause, it was just an agreement that allowed them to sell our kits under their label."

Toteff did a number of hot rod kits that appeared first as AMT products. "We did a couple models of some show cars that were well received. There was Joe Wilhelm's *Wild Dream*, a custom T-bucket, and Don Tognotti's *King T*." The Tognotti T was the 1964 winner of the "America's Most Beautiful Roadster" trophy at the Oakland Roadster Show. In addition to the two T's, AMT picked up the *Car Craft Dream Rod*.

"The *Dream Rod* was Bill Cushenberry's car," says Toteff. "*Car Craft* magazine hired him to build it. We worked to get the rights to produce it as a model, and then AMT picked it up."

AMT also released a 1928 Ford Model A Tudor sedan based on MPC tooling. "We really went all out on that sedan. It had opening doors and steerable front wheels. It was a nice model."

After AMT did its production run, MPC was free to release the kits on their own. "On a couple of cars," Toteff says, " we didn't change much, like the Wilhelm car. But I didn't want to release the

Some of MPC's best early kits were first released by AMT after George Toteff left AMT to start MPC. This 1928 Model A sedan was released by AMT in 1964, but was actually designed and tooled by MPC.

same kits as AMT, so we converted them to something else."

As an example, the 1928 Ford sedan was modified into a kit that offered builders the option of a pickup truck or a "woody" station wagon in a kit called *The Wild Ones.* Unfortunately, MPC didn't save original tooling components at the time. "That sedan body tool was probably modified into the wagon," Toteff says. "I had no plans to release that kit again in the AMT version, so I think that insert is probably gone."

While AMT marketed several of MPC's early kits under the agreement, it didn't take all of them. "The first kit we did under our own label was a 1964 Corvette. AMT already had one, so we offered ours with lots of extra parts, so you could make a drag version with working suspension."

Once he struck out on his own, Toteff and the designers at MPC worked with *Hot Rod* magazine to produce models based on Tom Medley's famous cartoon character, Stroker McGurk.

"Surfing was really big, so we designed this surfboard with a blown Chevy engine on it, and we tooled a little Stroker character to go with it," Toteff says. "We did several Stroker kits."

MPC developed a cadre of custom consultants early, based on Toteff's experiences at AMT. "Carl Casper was one of the first people we

Once AMT's run of the kit was completed, MPC engineers recut the tooling to produce a "woody" station wagon and pickup. The *Wild Ones* was a 1966 MPC release which featured *Hot Curl,* a California surfer's mascot. *Rick Hanmore*

worked with, and we did models of several of his cars," Toteff says. "The first one, I think, was that phone booth."

In 1964, Carl Casper was touring car shows with his *Phone Booth T.* The car was conceived as a pun based on a popular term for a Model T coupe with a stock roof. Because they were so tall and thin, hot rodders referred to them as "phone booths." Casper took that concept one step farther, and built a T chassis that carried a real telephone booth complete with pay phone.

"It was kind of goofy," says Toteff, "but show cars made popular kits. It did real well."

By 1966, Toteff had moved completely away from AMT. "We worked pretty hard to be self-contained. I didn't want to have to farm out any work to anyone else.

"We had our own design and engineering section, our own model makers, our own toolmaking department and mold shop, and our own production equipment. We even did our own shipping and distribution. It was just like an automotive factory in miniature.

"We even did our styling like the big car companies. Our patterns were done in clay first, then cast in fiberglass. I think we got better detail because of that."

A number of AMT employees followed Toteff to MPC after the company was established. Among them were designers Phil Sheldon and

As part of their popular *Gangbusters* series of vintage cars, MPC released a 1932 Chevy that offered both cabriolet and sedan delivery versions. MPC touted the model as the first "9-in-1" kit.

Bill Depuy. "Bill had been with AMT almost as long as I had. In fact, we've worked together off and on for almost 50 years," says Toteff.

"I was glad to have them. They weren't graduate engineers. They were *kit* engineers with years of experience, but they were car people, too. They liked cars, and that was more important."

Another person who followed Toteff to MPC was customizer George Barris. "George was with us by about 1967 or 1968, I guess. He worked in the same capacity as he had at AMT, as a consultant. He also built some full-sized cars for us, too."

Like Monogram, MPC decided early that full-sized versions of some of their models made great advertising. Accordingly, he contracted with several custom car builders to build cars based on MPC model kits.

Bill Depuy, who started with AMT in 1960, saw several of his model designs recreated in full size. "I remember Phil Sheldon and George telling us that they could teach anybody to do the drawings," he says. "But they wanted you to like the cars.

"George really inspired all the stuff that went on," Depuy recalls. "He liked to have fun, but he worked hard and he expected you to do that, too."

After he moved to MPC in 1964, one of Depuy's first projects was a 1932 Chevy kit that

When AMT released its first Deuce kit in 1960, engineers designed it so modelers could build it in one version, then disassemble it to build another. MPC expanded on that idea with an entire line of hot rod kits called Switchers. This 1932 Ford offered roadster and coupe versions with extra parts to change the car at will.

was a part of the "Gangbusters" series. MPC did several vintage luxury cars from the 1920s in gangster motif, complete with liquor bottles and machine guns. Among them was the Chevy.

"We started out doing a sedan delivery," says Depuy. "Chevy didn't actually produce its own delivery bodies at the time, but we looked at some coach-built designs and said, 'Okay, what if?' We came up with the model that way.

"It was supposed to be a paddy wagon but we added a cabriolet body to the kit so you could build it a couple of different ways, too. And since it was a Chevy, we included a new Chevy V-8 with custom wheels and other hot rod parts."

Zingers were a series of 1/32-scale models with 1/20-scale engines. MPC had five full-sized replicas built by Chuck Miller and Steve Tansy to promote the model kits. This Volkswagen Beetle is equipped with a blown Chrysler Hemi.

As with other MPC tools, the 1932 Chevy was in production for about two years, when it was modified. "There was this dumb daytime TV show called *Dark Shadows* about a vampire," says Depuy. "We did a figure model of the main character, Barnabas Collins.

"Then somebody decided that a Barnabas hot rod would be a good companion model. They retooled that little Chevy sedan delivery into *Barnabas' Vampire Van*, and really screwed it up," he says. "I never really forgave them for that one."

As with everything else, Toteff had his own way of developing new products. "We didn't have a marketing committee," Depuy says. "The engineers and production people would get together with George and with Joe Stahovec, who was vice president for engineering.

Movie and TV cars were as prominent at MPC as they were at AMT. Among the best-known MPC show car models was this replica of Dean Jeffries' *Monkeemobile*. Based on a 1966 Pontiac GTO, the car was used by the Monkees band on its popular TV series and for personal appearances.

"You might jot down a few notes on some idea you had. We'd present those, and if George liked them we'd develop them further."

Sometimes the creative process could be even looser than that. "I remember one time, I was goofing around at my design table during lunch," Depuy recalls. "We had just completed some design work under contract with Airfix, the British model company. I had some test shots of an old sailing ship I had done for them.

"At the same time, we had just released a model of the *Beverly Hillbillies* truck. Barris had built a hot rod version for one segment of the show, so we offered both the original and the hot rod in our kit.

"I had one of those on my table, and I started cutting away at the ship hull to see if I could make it fit on the truck chassis. That's when George walked by.

"He looked at me," Depuy laughs, "and he said, 'What the hell is that?' I explained what I was doing, and he told me to finish it and bring it to the new products meeting later in the week. I didn't think he was serious."

Toteff was serious. "I liked creative ideas," he says. "I was willing to try things that were different. Even weird stuff, sometimes."

Depuy glued the ship-truck together and set in on the table at the next product meeting. "I remember somebody said, 'No, George,' when

Another of MPC's famous drag car kits was the wild Marcellus & Borsch *Winged Express,* a 1923 T fuel altered. MPC also released this chassis with a Bantam body to create a series of altered roadsters. *Bill Coulter*

they saw it," Depuy recalls. "But George liked it, and we did it. We did some pretty strange models, but I think that ship car was about the dumbest.

"Harry Bradley did some consulting work for us," he says. "They sent it out to Harry and he refined it and came up with this pirate motif. So we called it the *Jolly Rodger.*

"It started out as a joke, but it sold. At that time, you could sell almost anything you came up with, as long as you maintained the quality."

By the mid-1970s, Toteff sold his controlling interest in MPC to Fundimensions, a branch of General Mills. MPC continued to produce some of the most popular model kits of the era, and manufactured a significant number of the dealer promotional models available from Chrysler Corporation, Ford, and GM. Consequently, MPC released dozens of annual Detroit releases based on that promo tooling. Some of the most significant muscle car model kits of the period came from MPC—Chevy Super Sports, GTOs, Dodge Chargers, 'Cudas, and Mustangs.

MPC also focused on drag racing models, releasing kits of racing teams including Roger Lindamood's *Color Me Gone* funny car and Don Carlton's prostock Plymouth Duster, *Mopar Missile.*

# George Barris, King of the Kustomizers

Although George Barris is most often identified with AMT Corporation, he actually started his consulting career at Revell. "Royel and Lew Glaser contacted me in '56 or '57 about some of their kits," he says. "The first model kit I worked on was their '56 Buick."

Barris signed an exclusive contract with AMT in 1961 and served as a consultant there for five years. AMT also produced nearly a dozen models of his full-sized cars.

MPC, though, probably produced more models of Barris cars than any company. That arrangement included cars Barris had already built, as well as a number of cars he built to MPC specifications.

"I built several cars that were based on their kits," he says. "They did the model first before I ever built the big car."

Among the Barris cars that AMT produced were the *Beverly Hillbillies* truck, the Stutz Bearcat from the TV show *Bearcats*, the *Bed Buggy*, and a wild three-wheeled custom called the *Ricksha*. One of the most spectacular cars was the *Raiders' Coach*, a custom stagecoach pulled by a pair of GTO engines, which Barris built for Paul Revere and the Raiders. MPC's kit included miniature figures for all the band members, too.

Other collaborations included the *Hardhat Hauler*, the *Mail Truck*, and the *Ice Cream Truck*. All told, MPC and Barris collaborated on more than 20 model kits.

Barris had another distinction as well. Of all the custom car builders who worked as consultants for the model companies, Barris had models produced by more companies than any other: Aurora, AMT, MPC, Revell, Monogram, and Testors. According to Mark Gustavson, curator of the National Model Car Builders' Museum, the model companies produced more than 30 Barris cars between 1956 and 1976.

"It doesn't matter whether he was working on real cars or models," Gustavson says. "When it comes to sheer numbers, he really *is* the King of the Kustomizers."

MPC also released the Milner dragster, which appeared in *More American Graffiti*. This was actually a release of the *Ramchargers* chassis with new decals. The model also featured a Bantam coupe body to build a fuel coupe. *Bill Coulter*

MPC's hot rod kits from this period were primarily modified versions of previous kits. The company developed a practice of combining components from several different kits to produce an "all-new model." In 1975, it did just that to introduce two kits that tied in with the recently formed National Street Rod Association. The *Li'l Evil T* kit was a combination of parts from MPC's original Tognotti *King T* with the chassis components from the Switchers 1927 T coupe kit.

MPC's earlier Switchers 1932 Ford sedan kit was modified slightly to produce a 1932 Ford sedan delivery in the same series.

At the same time, a third Switchers kit was revised to produce a model of perhaps the most famous hot rod of all time: John Milner's yellow Deuce coupe from the George Lucas film, *American Graffiti*. To tie in with the second film, *More American Graffiti*, MPC added bobbed fenders and chrome wheels to its 1932 Ford coupe Switchers kit. The resulting model was not particularly accurate. In fact, MPC graphic artists airbrushed photos of the actual car to remove the Man-A-Fre four-carburetor intake, and replaced it with the dual four-barrel intake that was included in the kit.

One of MPC's more interesting kits consisted of a 1/10-scale engine that was accompanied by a caricature figure of a famous driver. In addition to this Don Garlits 426 Hemi, MPC produced a model of Shirley Muldowney. *Bill Coulter*

In spite of the inaccuracies, the *American Graffiti* coupe kit is one of the most desirable of MPC's collectible hot rod kits.

A second model was issued to tie in with the film, as well. MPC revised one of its earlier top fuel dragster kits and added decals to mimic Milner's dragster from *More American Graffiti.* Based on more detailed tooling than the coupe, the dragster was a better, more accurate model of the actual car. In addition, the kit included a much-modified Austin Bantam body, which allowed modelers to build a fuel coupe. Like the coupe, the Milner dragster kit is avidly sought by collectors.

The Ertl Company purchased MPC in 1985. Ertl continued to run both AMT and MPC brands until 1988, when it decided to cancel the MPC name for new kit production.

"It came down to the kit boxes," says designer John Mueller. "MPC's boxes were slightly bigger, so you could only get 10 boxes in

Although MPC as a brand has disappeared, many of its models have shown up with AMT's logo in recent years. AMT's *Connoisseur Classics* series reintroduced many of MPC's old Gangbusters kits, including the 1932 Chevy cabriolet. Dragster kits with original box art surfaced in AMT's Buyers' Choice program, while several MPC 1/20 show car kits reappeared in AMT's 1998 catalog.

a standard AMT shipping carton. AMT kit boxes fit 12 to a carton. Since they were switching to all-AMT boxes, they just decided to release all their new kits with AMT's logo, and MPC disappeared."

As Revell-Monogram did earlier, AMT/Ertl developed a series of limited-release kits that were provided only to hobby shops and kit dealers. The Buyers' Choice program included a number of vintage MPC kits, rereleased with original box art and duplicates of the original instruction sheets and decals. Among the more popular rereleases were the Marcellus & Borsch T altered drag car, *Winged Express,* and the famous *Ramchargers* top fuel dragster.

Original MPC kits today are highly prized by collectors and bring good prices in many cases. George Toteff believes that popularity is a combination of kit quality and subject matter. "We worked hard to produce a good product," he says. "We were the first ones to use Elverson jewelry engraving machines for our detail engraving. We never cheated on the details. That's why MPC took off the way it did."

# chapter five

# Companies Great and Small

It's just this treasure trove of old hot rod kits.
— *Matt Thrasher, marketing specialist, Lindberg*

Revell, AMT, Monogram, and MPC were known as the "Big Four" in the American hobby industry, but they weren't the only companies producing hot rod models.

More than a dozen firms manufactured model kits in the United States during the 1960s. Though most weren't as big or as prominent as the "Big Four," they nonetheless turned out some fun models.

Most are no longer in business. Others were absorbed into larger companies through corporate buyouts and mergers. Here are a few of them.

**Aurora**

Aurora was a New York–based model kit company best known for model kits of famous movie monsters, and for its Model Motoring and A/FX HO race car sets. However, it produced nearly two dozen hot rod kits, primarily in 1/32 scale. Aurora also did two early Ford kits, a 1934 Ford and a 1922 Ford T, in 1/25 scale, that were released in "double kit" form with a factory stock model and a second hot rod model.

Hawk Model Company is best known for its Weirdos kits. Designed by William Campbell, the Weirdos were immensely popular with preteen boys. Subject matter included cars, surfing, sports, and even a rock band. *Bill Coulter*

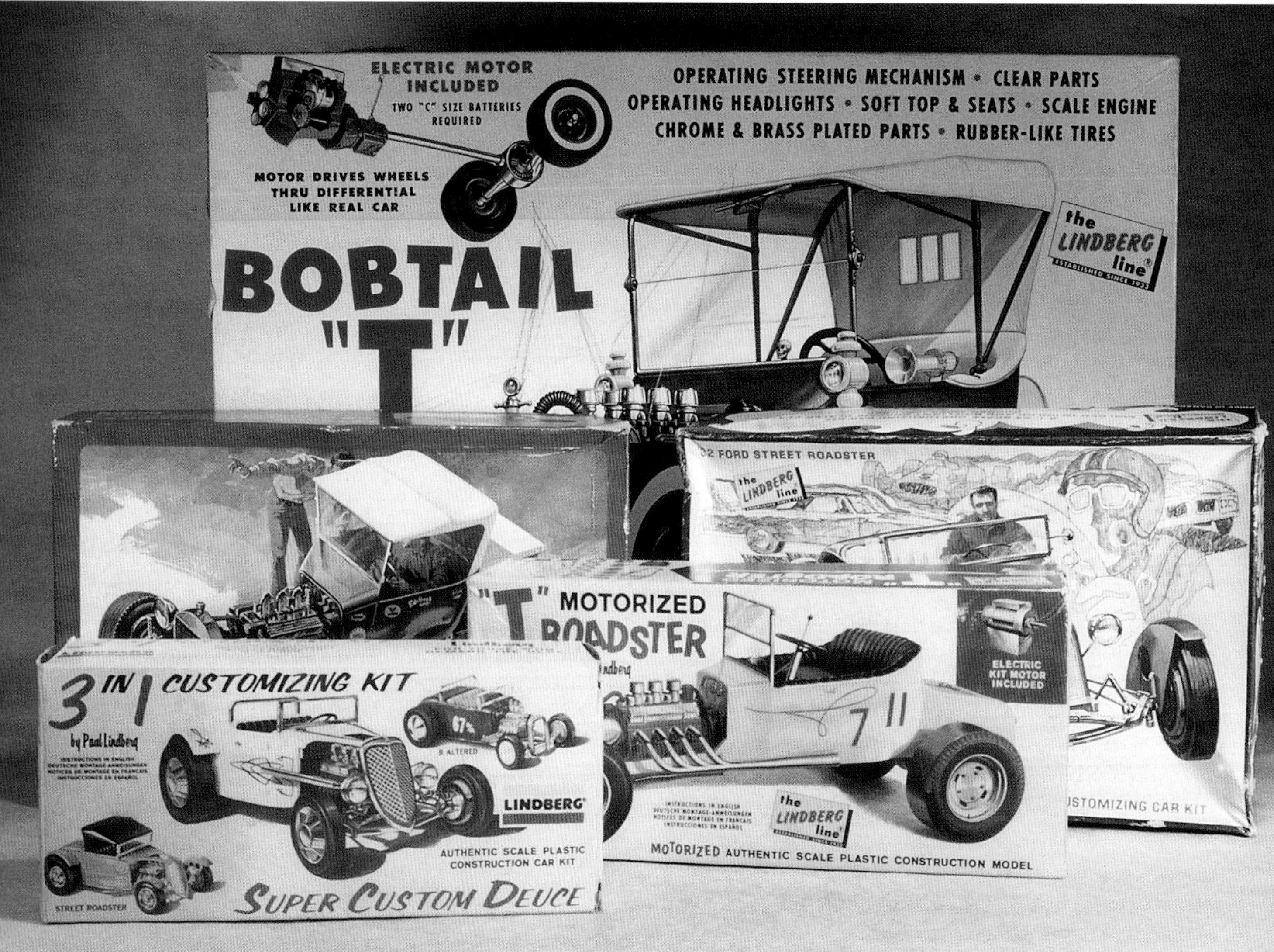


Lindberg released kits in a wide range of scales. Their 3-in-1 Customizing Kit of the *Super Custom Deuce* was in 1/32 scale. The *Tee Wagon* and the *Speed Freak* 1932 Ford were in 1/24 scale, while the *Motorized T Roadster* was in 1/27.5 scale. The big *Bobtail T* in back is in 1/8 scale.

In 1977, Aurora's assets were sold to Monogram Models. During transport from Long Island to Illinois, the freight cars carrying Aurora's tools derailed, irreparably damaging many of the mold tools. Some survived and are still produced by Monogram today. However, none of the original hot rod kits were ever re-issued, suggesting that those tools were damaged too badly to repair.

## Lindberg

Paul Lindberg started his model company in 1934. The original "Lindberg Line" was primarily wooden airplane and ship models. After World War II, he expanded into plastics, and by 1960, was producing a wide range of model car kits. Lindberg produced hot rod model kits in more different scales than any other model company. Its kits ranged from 1/87 (HO model railroad scale) through 1/32, 1/27, 1/24, 1/16, 1/12, and 1/8. Lindberg released hot rod kits in all of those scales from 1960 to 1970.

Lindberg continues to produce model kits and has re-issued a number of the '60s hot rods. In addition, they have introduced some new tools in recent years that were lauded by the hobby press. Those include '64 Dodge Super Stock sedans and a '53 Ford Crestline Victoria, the first detailed model kit of that car ever released.

In 1999, Lindberg realized that it had a huge warehouse full of kits that no one had seen in 30 years. The company began a program to re-release many of the old Lindberg and Pyro hot rod kits through hobby shops. According to Matt Thrasher, a marketing specialist for the company, "It's just this treasure trove of old hot rod kits."

## Hawk

Hawk's biggest claim to fame was its fabulous Weirdos line of hot rod monsters created by William Campbell. Weirdos were immensely popular with adolescent boys and sold so well that Hawk released nearly two dozen different

One of Aurora's rarest kits is the 1934 Ford double kit. Each kit provided enough parts to build both an original 1934 coupe and a hot rod version. The hot rod featured chrome-plated cycle fenders.

By far, Aurora's largest hot rod kit series was available in 1/32 scale. The series offered subjects ranging from a tall T coupe to a 1929 Ford fire engine to a LaSalle hearse! Although they were smaller scale, Aurora's little hot rod kits were well detailed. *Rick Hanmore*

monster kits, with themes ranging from drag racing to surfing to sports, and even a Beatles spoof.

Hawk did few "serious" hot rod kits. In 1964, it produced a custom surfer's wagon that appeared to be a knock-off of AMT's *Surf Woody* kit. That model was released several times with different decals and names, including the *Wild Woody, Surf Wagon,* and the *Sandpiper.* Most of Hawk's tooling was purchased by the Testors Corporation in the mid 1980s. Testors rereleased nearly a dozen of the original *Weirdos* kits in 1994 and 1995.

### Eldon

Like Aurora, Eldon was best known for model race car sets and other toys. However, it produced a series of kits based on famous show cars of the era, primarily cars built by Bob Reisner. Reisner's twin-engined *Invader* won the 1964

*Rod & Custom* magazine was heavily involved in the model car hobby, mainly because of the efforts of editor Bill Neumann. From June 1964 until January 1965, *Rod & Custom Models* devoted its pages solely to model cars, such as this replica of the Mura Brothers' Willys drag pickup, built by hobby writer Don Emmons. The model still exists and is on loan to the National Model Car Builders' Museum.

# *Rod & Custom*

One of the major influences in the growth of model car building was not a model kit company. It was a magazine—a *car* magazine. *Rod & Custom* published articles on model cars as early as 1956. However, the coverage was spotty at best until a legendary confluence occurred. At about the time AMT released its customizing kits and the other companies scrambled to catch up, Petersen Publishing hired a new editor for the magazine. Bill Neumann came to *Rod & Custom* in 1961 as an established, successful builder of full-sized hot rods and customs.

He was also an avid model builder. Almost from the moment Neumann went to work, *R&C* began to cover model car building. Neumann hired one of the country's top modelers, Don Emmons, to write a regular column and encouraged other writers and staffers to contribute model-related articles, as well. Automotive artist Joe Henning was among those who wrote articles explaining how to duplicate famous cars.

In the spring of 1964, Petersen Publishing introduced a spin-off magazine called *Rod & Custom Models*. That magazine was packed with information on new products, hobby show coverage, model how-tos, and slot racing. After eight issues, the magazine was combined with *Rod & Custom* to produce a magazine called *Rod & Custom Cars & Models*. That experiment lasted only four issues. Early in 1966, Neumann left to pursue other ventures, and *Rod & Custom* dropped model coverage altogether.

Would the hobby have grown so large without *Rod & Custom*? It's safe to say that no other mainstream magazine devoted as much effort to the promotion of the model car hobby.

Mark Gustavson of the National Model Car Builders' Museum agrees. "Without the truly national forum that *Rod & Custom* provided, I don't think the hobby would have been nearly as popular as it was."

"America's Most Beautiful Roadster" trophy at the Oakland Roadster Show. Eldon released a kit of that car, as well as the *Milk Truck*, a custom C-cab, along with a model of a Reisner show car called the *Outhouse*, and a model of Joe Bailon's custom *Pink Panther* limousine.

**Industro-Motive Corporation**

Industro-Motive Corporation was a plastics manufacturer that concentrated on butter dishes and other utensils. In 1964, it hired Budd Anderson to develop a series of model car kits. Anderson did a remarkable group of mid-1960s Ford sports and Indy cars. He also designed a pair of 1948 Fords and a 1964 Volkswagen with a wild gasser racing version. Perhaps the most famous of his creations for IMC was a model of a wheel-standing Dodge pickup by Bill "Maverick" Golden, the *Little Red Wagon*. Many of IMC's tools were eventually purchased by Lindberg, and have been rereleased since 1990.

Budd Anderson moved from AMT to Industro-Motive Corporation in 1964. One of the models he designed was this 1963 Volkswagen. Extra parts provided a drag gasser option powered by a blown Chevy. *John Bowman*

Probably the best remembered of all of Budd Anderson's models for IMC was the *Little Red Wagon*. This model of the wheel-standing Dodge truck by Bill "Maverick" Golden also offered a stock version. *Bill Coulter*

Jo-Han Models of Detroit never did any classic hot rods, but it did offer custom versions of many American cars. This is a 1960 DeSoto, complete with spotlights, dual antennas, lakes pipes, flipper hubcaps, and fender skirts. *Rick Hanmore*

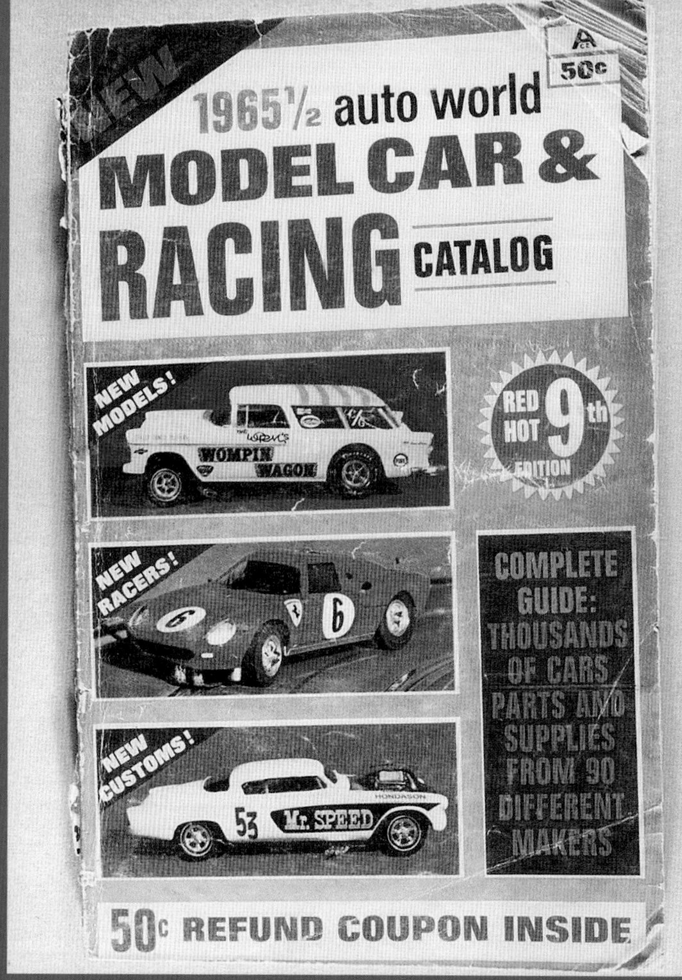


For 30 years beginning in 1958, the *Auto World* catalog brought model kits, paints, and detailing parts to front doors worldwide. The catalog was better stocked than any hobby shop, and offered products for scale model builders and slot car racers alike.

# *Auto World* and *Car Model*

For thousands of kids in America during the early 1960s, ordering by mail was the only way to get the newest kits and modeling supplies. And for nearly 30 years, the best place to mail order kits and supplies was *Auto World*. Started by A. M. Koveleski (Oscar) in 1958, the company offered supplies for model building, slot car racing, and even custom bicycles.

"We started out selling a couple of boxes of kits when we went to the races," Koveleski recalls. "I was racing sports cars all around New York and Pennsylvania at the time, and we would take some models with us wherever we went." Koveleski's father, Tony, had started manufacturing a line of model kits called "Li'l Old Timers" just after World War II. "I was around models all the time, so I carried them with me. People started asking, 'What else do you have, what else can you get?'"

Oscar realized the potential of this hobby sales business, and put together his first catalog in 1958. "From the beginning, we tried to offer more than just kits," he says. "We had all kinds of paint and tools, and lots of detailing supplies.

"So much of that was made to order for us, or we put it together ourselves with our own packaging. And we pulled all the orders, too, and did all the shipping with just a couple of people."

The business grew because of clever marketing. "We advertised in the magazines, but we also published our own catalog and arranged to have

Letters from *Auto World* customers prompted Oscar Koveleski to produce a model car magazine. *Car Model* offered several detailed projects for modelers to follow. R. A. Smith's 1940 Ford sedan, the *Crusader,* is considered one of the best models of the era. Several issues of the magazine followed the building process in 1963.

it sold on newsstands just like the magazines." That, he believes, was one of the major reasons for *Auto World*'s growth. "You could find the catalog almost anywhere."

By 1963, *Auto World* was fielding hundreds of letters from modelers asking for help with particular model techniques. "We looked at all that and decided to start a magazine. There really wasn't anything at the time, so we launched *Car Model*. And because our market was kids, we kept the price down, so they could afford it."

Initial issues sold for just 25 cents. Later, when the magazine format was enlarged, they increased the price to 35 cents.

"Our customers, those 12- to 15-year-old kids, they were participants, not only in the hobby but also in our business. They wanted to be a part of this, and that's why we were successful.

"By reading the kit instructions and our magazine articles, they learned to understand the parts of a car and the engineering behind cars and models both. There was a real educational value for a lot of kids.

"When they got older, they took that knowledge with them to full-sized cars," he says proudly. "There are a lot of auto designers, great mechanics, and race car drivers who used to be our customers."

Jo-Han offered some great drag racing models, primarily pro stocks and funny cars. The kits were equipped with some of the most detailed racing engines done in the period. Their Logghe racing chassis was considered among the best in the industry.

## Jo-Han

Jo-Han Models was originally called Ideal Models. A problem arose with trademarks, though, when Ideal Toy Company protested the similarity. In response, founder John Haenle combined parts of his own name ("Jo" from John and "Han" from Haenle) to create a new name — Jo-Han. Jo-han concentrated primarily on models of contemporary American cars, and produced promotional models for Chrysler Corporation and General Motors from 1955 until 1978.

While Jo-Han never actually produced hot rods in the strictest sense, they did manufacture some great drag racing kits beginning in the early 1960s. By 1972, they had released top quality kits of funny cars and pro/stocks, featuring such drag racing greats as "Dyno" Don Nicholson, Gene Snow, and Mickey Thompson. Their drag kits were well-detailed and featured remarkable engine compartments; the funny cars rode on intricate Logghe chassis.

Jo-Han was purchased by an investment group called Seville Enterprises in the early '90s. Seville continues to produce a few of Jo-Han's drag racing kits, including Mustang and Pinto funny cars. Much of the older tooling, however, is said to have been discarded prior to Seville's purchase.

Palmer Plastics wasn't known for doing hot rod models, but it did release one T-bucket kit about 1962. The *Tiger Cat,* produced in 1/32 scale, featured a surprising level of detail.

Eldon was recognized as a manufacturer of slot car racing sets, but it also did a series of 1/25-scale model kits based on famous show cars, primarily those built by Bob Reisner. These two, the *Outhouse* and the *Milk Truck*, are actually Japanese reissues of the original Eldon kits.

## Palmer Plastics

Palmer Plastics was another New York–based model company that produced low-priced model car kits until about 1970. Many of its kits were hastily conceived and were toylike in their execution. However, around 1962, Palmer Plastics did produce one commendable hot rod kit in 1/32 scale. The *Tiger Cat* was a T-bucket with a Chevy V-8 and Olds spinner hubcaps. The model was available only for a short time, then disappeared. Pyro bought Palmer in the early 1970s and were themselves purchased by Lindberg in about 1974. To date, none of their hot rod kits have been re-released.

## Pyro Plastics

Pyro Plastics manufactured hot rod model kits in 1/12 and 1/16 scale. Like Palmer, it was based in New York. Among the best of its kits was a 1/12-scale Fiat drag coupe and the *Tee-N-T*, a 1/16-scale kit with multiple versions. Pyro kits were not on the same level as AMT or MPC kits, but were well done, especially for the price. Pyro was purchased by Lindberg in the late 1970s.

Most of the smaller model companies have disappeared. Lindberg, however, has continued to introduce many vintage kits, including AMT's original 1934 Ford pickup. New companies include Galaxie Limited, with its Monogram dragster reissues and its all-new 1948 Chevy kit. Polar Lights, a division of Playing Mantis, has released replicas of vintage Aurora kits, as well as an all-new series of vintage funny cars.

# Appendix 1: The Aftermarket

So what's new? Much has changed in just the last 20 years. All those kids who built models in the 1960s and 1970s rediscovered their hobby in the 1980s and 1990s. Consequently, the model kit hobby is stronger than ever.

The major development for model car builders is a strong aftermarket composed of small manufacturers who produce conversion and detailing kits. Hot rod and drag racing kits are available in hand-cast resin and white metal. Detailing kits range from prewired distributors to photoetched engine and interior details. Modelers can purchase machined wheels, decals for famous race cars, and separate tire sets.

The aftermarket is such that if you can think of a model or a part, you can probably find someone who manufactures it, no matter how obscure the item.

Although all of the old model magazines are out of production, a strong newcomer emerged in their wake, and it has covered the hobby for more than 20 years. *Scale Auto Enthusiast* is considered a major factor in the resurgence of the model car hobby in all categories, especially among adult builders.

The diecast market has also developed hot rod model kits. In addition to factory-finished models, manufacturers have released prepainted, simple model kits in many forms. Check with your local hobby shop to see what's available. If you don't have a hobby shop, try your local newsstand to get a copy of *Scale Auto Enthusiast.* And for more information, check the Web. Many shops and clubs have Websites with great photos and other information. We've included some addresses here if you want to look further.

As the millennium turns, the future for hot rod models looks more fun than ever.

# Sources

Scale Auto Enthusiast magazine
21027 Crossroads Circle
Waukesha, Wisconsin 53187
http://www.scaleautomag.com

Kalmbach Books (how-to model books)
21027 Crossroads Circle, PO Box 986
Waukesha, Wisconsin 53187-0986
http://books.kalmbach.com

The National Model Car Builders' Museum
353 East 400 South
Salt Lake City, Utah 84111
http://www.xmission.com/~msgsl/nmcbm

The Modelhaus (resin kits and parts)
5480 Traughber Road
Decatur, Illinois 62521
http://www.modelhaus.com

Replicas & Miniatures Company of Maryland (resin hot rod parts, engine parts)
317 Roosevelt Ave, SW
Glen Burnie, Maryland 21061

R&D Unique (cast metal hot rod chassis, engines, and detail parts)
17113 S.E. 149th St.
Renton, Washington 98059
http://hometown.aol.com/RnDUnique

Hobby Heaven (new and vintage kits)
PO Box 3229
Grand Rapids, Michigan 49501
http://www.modelcarkits.com

Wheat's Nostalgia (vintage model car kits)
216 Tech Road
Pittsburgh, Pennsylvania 15205
http://members.aol.com/wheatsnost

Galaxie, Limited (vintage Monogram reproductions, all-new 1948 Chevy kits)
PO Box 655
Butler, Wisconsin 53007

Detail Master (photoetched parts and detailing supplies)
PO Box 2815
Purcellville, Virginia
20134-2815
http://www.detailmaster.com

Model Car Garage (photoetched parts and detailing supplies)
2908 SE Bella Rd
Port St. Lucie, Florida 34984
http://www.modelcargarage.com

Model Empire (current and vintage kits)
7116 W. Greenfield Av.
West Allis, Wisconsin 53214
http://www.modelempire-usa.com

The Good Stuff (resin kits and parts for drag racing cars)
PO Box 131351
Roseville, Minnesota 55113-0012

Modelers have an enormous range of new products available. In this photo are resin cast kits, metal kits, factory-finished diecast models, decals, and detailing parts ranging from wheel sets to photo-etched emblems.

# Appendix 2: Model Kit Value Guide

A major collector's market for model cars developed in the last 20 years, and several dealers specialize in vintage collectible kits. Be prepared, though, to bring a fat wallet. A lot of those old $1.49 model kits sell today for well over $100!

For a book like this, the problem with trying to place a value on collectible model kits is that the price guide will be out of date before the book reaches the shelves. As is the case with all "baby boomer" collectibles, prices for vintage model car kits have soared. Hot rod kits appear to be some of the most popular and, consequently, the highest priced.

Here's a rough idea what you should expect to pay for mint, unbuilt examples of the models shown in this book. For built models, figure about half of the listed price. Keep in mind that many of these kits have been reissued several times over the years. In other words, be careful and try to avoid paying a hundred bucks for 10 bucks' worth of plastic.

**AMT**
1963 Buick 3-in-1 Advanced Customized Kit 125.00
1932 Ford Deuce Coupe (original edition) 75.00
1932 Ford roadster 60.00
1940 Ford coupe 50.00
1925 Ford Double T (original edition) 125.00
Double Dragster 100.00
1940 Willys Coupe/Pickup 75.00
1957 Thunderbird (Styline edition) 70.00
Don Garlits' *Wynn's Jammer* top fuel dragster (original edition) 100.00
1929 Ford Model A/*Ala Kart* double kit (original edition) 180.00
1928 Ford Model A sedan 125.00
*Pirahna* dragster 175.00

**Aurora**
1934 Ford coupe double kit 175.00
1922 Ford sedan (1/32 original) 40.00

**Eldon**
Bob Reisner's *Outhouse* showcar (original) 75.00

**Hawk**
Weirdos *Digger* 25.00
*Surf Wagon/Sandpiper* 50.00

**IMC**
1963 Volkswagen Beetle 75.00
*Li'l Red Wagon* (original) 60.00

**Jo-Han**
1960 DeSoto 75.00
1971 Ford Maverick Dyno Don prostock 125.00

**Monogram**
Hot Rod (original edition) 100.00
1932 Ford Deuce Sport Coupe 125.00
Sizzler dragster 150.00
1929 Ford pickup *Blue Beetle* (original edition) 75.00
1930 Ford A phaeton hot rod *Red Chariot* 100.00
1934 Ford coupe/cabriolet (original edition) 100.00
Darryl Starbird's *Predicta* (original edition) 75.00
*Big T* (original edition) 350.00
*Big Tub* 500.00
*Big Deuce* (original edition) 250.00
Tom Daniel's *Tijuana Taxi* 250.00
Tom Daniel's *Red Baron* (1/12 scale) 125.00

**MPC**
*Wild Ones* 1928 Ford woody/pickup (original edition) 70.00
1932 Chevy sedan delivery/cabriolet Gangbusters 125.00
1932 Ford roadster/coupe Switchers 75.00
Dean Jeffries' *Monkeemobile* (original) 70.00
*Beverly Hillbillies Truck* 225.00
*Jolly Rodger* 190.00
George Barris' *Ice Cream Truck* 60.00
Mr. Gasket Mustang gasser 150.00
1971 Plymouth Duster *Mopar Missile* pro stock 175.00
*American Graffiti* John Milner 1932 Ford coupe 175.00
*American Graffiti* top fuel dragster 150.00

**Palmer**
*Tiger Cat* T-bucket (1/32) 25.00

**Revell**
*Highway Pioneers* V-8 Hot Rod (1/32) 45.00
1956 Buick Customizing Kit (1/32) 70.00
Ed Roth's *Outlaw* (original) 75.00
1956 Ford F-100 pickup (original) 60.00
1941 Willys Stone-Woods-Cook (original) 60.00
1932 Ford sedan Bob Tindle's *Orange Crate* 100.00
Ed Roth's *Rat Fink* (light-up eyes) 125.00
*Meter Cheater* custom taxi 90.00
1951 Anglia gasser 45.00

George Barris collaborated with MPC designers on more than a dozen kits. This one is the *Ice Cream Truck*. MPC often modified existing tooling to produce what appeared to be all-new kits. This model was based on an earlier design by Joe Wilhelm.

MPC released a series of kits in conjunction with the newly formed National Street Rod Association in the early 1970s. These two, the *Li'l Evil T* and the *Keep On Truckin'* 32 Ford, were based on MPC's earlier Switcher kits.

# index